Experiencing Disability Stigma in Ghana

Experiencing Disability Stigma in Ghana

Impact on Individuals and Caregivers

Magnus Mfoafo-M'Carthy, Jeff Grischow, and Festus Moasun

LEXINGTON BOOKS
Lanham • Boulder • New York • London

Published by Lexington Books
An imprint of The Rowman & Littlefield Publishing Group, Inc.
4501 Forbes Boulevard, Suite 200, Lanham, Maryland 20706
www.rowman.com

86-90 Paul Street, London EC2A 4NE

British Library Cataloguing in Publication Information Available

Library of Congress Cataloging-in-Publication Data

Names: Mfoafo-M'Carthy, Magnus, author. | Grischow, Jeff D. (Jeff Douglas), 1965– author. | Moasun, Festus, author.
Title: Experiencing disability stigma in Ghana : impact on individuals and caregivers / edited by Magnus Mfoafo-M'Carthy, Jeff Grischow, and Festus Moasun.
Description: Lanham : Lexington Books, 2023. | Includes bibliographical references and index. | Summary: "This book explores stigma and discrimination associated with disability and mental health in Ghana. In conversations with caregivers and persons with disabilities, the authors examine the socio-cultural challenges that undermine treatment and support for these individuals and provide recommendations for improved policy and practice"— Provided by publisher.
Identifiers: LCCN 2023044469 (print) | LCCN 2023044470 (ebook) | ISBN 9781666905809 (cloth) | ISBN 9781666905816 (ebook)
Subjects: LCSH: People with disabilities—Ghana—Social conditions. | Caregivers—Ghana—Social conditions. | Stigma (Social psychology)—Ghana. | Discrimination against people with disabilities—Ghana. | Discrimination against caregivers—Ghana.
Classification: LCC HV1559.G4 M36 2023 (print) | LCC HV1559.G4 (ebook) | DDC 362.404109667—dc23/eng/20230921
LC record available at https://lccn.loc.gov/2023044469
LC ebook record available at https://lccn.loc.gov/2023044470

We dedicate this book to all participants who shared their life stories, and to all those who continue to endure different challenges based on their disabilities.

Contents

Acknowledgments ix

List of Abbreviations xi

PART I: SETTING THE CONTEXT **1**

Introduction 3

1 The History of Disability in Ghana 15

PART II: EXPERIENCING DISABILITY AND DISABILITY STIGMA **37**

2 Culture and Disability in Ghana 39

3 Religion, Spirituality, and Mental Illness in Ghana 59

4 Stigma, Discrimination, and Impact on Individuals with Disabilities 75

5 Stigma, Discrimination, and Impact on Ghanaian Families 91

PART III: THE WAY FORWARD **113**

6 Doing Disability Research in Ghana: Lessons Learned and Recommendations 115

Conclusion 125

References 129

Index 147

About the Authors 153

Acknowledgments

This book is the result of scholarly research conducted in Ghana over a long span of time. The research involved engagements with multiple communities across the country. For this reason, we acknowledge and are thankful to community leaders, community members, and members of the disability community who gracefully welcomed and supported us in field data collection. We are especially thankful to persons with disabilities, family members, and caregivers who spared their time and energies with us, but more importantly, who graciously shared their experiences, some of which were harrowing to them. We are thankful to all the research assistants who had to travel to sometimes very remote communities to interview research participants.

We wish to express our sincerest gratitude to the publishers, Lexington Books, for reposing confidence in our project and agreeing to publish this book. We are especially grateful to Shelby Russell, who began the journey with us, and to Sydney Wedbush, who took over from Shelby along the way and coordinated the project to its successful completion.

We would like to acknowledge the support of our respective families. Magnus would like to warmly appreciate his wife, Stella, and their daughters, Daisy and Michelle. Jeff thanks Yvette, Sydney, and Theo, and Festus thanks his wife, Yvonne, and their children, Tilibe, Belma, and Afram. We are deeply indebted to them for their encouragement and support.

Finally, we would like to acknowledge the Social Sciences and Humanities Research Council (SSHRC) of Canada for providing funding for the research from which a large part of the information for this book was obtained.

List of Abbreviations

ADA	Americans with Disabilities Act
AHC	Ad Hoc Committee
ARC	Accra Rehabilitation Center
BCDOP	British Council of Organizations of Disabled People
CBR	Community Based Rehabilitation
CPP	Convention People's Party
CRPD	Convention on the Rights of Persons with Disabilities
DPI	Disabled People's International
DPOs	Disabled People's Organization
ECA	Economic Commission for Africa
GAB	Ghana Association of the Blind
GES	Ghana Education Service
GFD	Ghana Federation of the Disabled (now Ghana Federation of Disability Organisations)
GSB	Ghana Society for the Blind
GSPD	Ghana Society of the Physically Disabled
HRW	Human Rights Watch
IE	Inclusive Education
ILO	International Labour Organization
IYDP	International Year of Disabled People
LI	Legislative Instrument
NAD	Norwegian Association of the Disabled
NGOs	Non-Governmental Organizations
NHIA	National Health Insurance Authority
NHIS	National Health Insurance Scheme
NORAD	Norwegian Agency for Development Cooperation
NSPP	National Social Protection Policy

OTC	Orthopaedic Training Centre
PAR	Participatory Action Research
PNDC	Provisional National Defence Council
RAVI	Rights and Voice Initiative
RI	Rehabilitation International
SFMRA	Society of Friends of the Mentally Retarded Association
SHIA	Persons International Aid Association
SSHRC	Sciences Research and Humanities Council of Canada
UN	United Nations
UNDESA	United Nations Division for Social Policy Development, and Department of Economic and Social Affairs
UNDSPD	United Nations Division for Social Policy and Development
UNESCO	United Nations Educational, Scientific and Cultural Organization
UNICEF	United Nations Children's Fund
UPIAS	Union of the Physically Impaired Against Segregation
USA	United States of America
WHO	World Health Organization
YMCA	Young Men's Christian Association

Part I

SETTING THE CONTEXT

Introduction

This book explores stigma and discrimination toward disability in Ghana, as experienced by persons with disabilities and their caregivers. According to the World Health Organization (WHO), "disability results from the interaction between individuals with a health condition. . .with personal and environmental factors including negative attitudes, inaccessible transportation and public buildings, and limited social support" (World Health Organization, 2023). Under this definition, health conditions can include diseases and physical impairments that have a substantial adverse impact on a person's ability to participate in day-to-day undertakings. These impairments include challenges affecting senses such as sight and hearing, mobility and physical coordination. Mental and psychological impairments may include learning disabilities, mental illness, memory problems, and difficulty with concentration. Faced with impairments and disabling social attitudes, persons with disabilities worldwide aspire to live, work, and contribute to well-being, and live in harmony with other members of their communities. These individuals have the same inkling as others to be educated, develop their capabilities, and play a significant role in society.

There are numerous individuals with disabilities, including Ghanaians, who have contributed immensely to their communities worldwide in politics, the arts, science, research, and many other realms.[1] However, in certain parts of the Global South, persons with disabilities are discriminated against severely, leading to social marginalization and ostracization. They are disowned, abandoned, and even killed in some instances. In Ghana, this mistreatment is heightened because many Ghanaians attribute the causes of disability to curses based on the sins of their predecessors, witchcraft, and other forms of evil. The analysis that follows seeks to illuminate and analyze this important issue. It forms part of a larger collaborative project over the past six years, during which time the authors have engaged in a series of research projects on disability issues in Ghana. Our research has focused on understanding how disability stigma is perceived by Ghanaians and how they cope with it. Based on interviews conducted in Ghana, this book specifically assesses the roots of stigma and discrimination and their social and economic impact on individuals with disabilities and their caregivers. The inclusion of caregivers fills a major research gap because few studies have included their voices despite the extreme burdens they face alongside individuals in their care. In total, we interviewed 120 individuals and their caregivers in four study areas across Ghana: Accra, the capital of Ghana; Kumasi, the cultural capital in the Ashanti; Cape Coast and Takoradi, in the Central and Western Regions, respectively; and several locations in the Northern Region.

In order to establish the context of our research sites, it is important to provide a brief socioeconomic and cultural overview of the country. According to Ghana Statistical Services, Ghana's population reached 29.6 million in 2018 (2018). This shows a remarkable growth in population since independence, when the population was around six million. Since the country's colonial period prior to 1957, urban areas, which include the capital city, Accra, have customarily been supplied with amenities, which has led to the rapid development of these communities in comparison to the rural areas. This development has resulted in the migration of youth and adults to urban areas in search of greener pastures. Thus, in contrast to the Savannah regions in the northern parts of the country, the urban cities tend to attract more people due to the availability of jobs and the propensity for better education and modern ways of life. According to the World Bank, Ghana attained middle-income country status in 2010 with the discovery of oil (World Bank, 2011). The economy has steadily grown by 7 percent per average each year since then. Despite the steady economic growth, inequality continues to increase as poverty remains prevalent, with unemployment at its zenith. The country's inequality has been attributed to the uneven distribution of wealth, particularly among politicians who are perceived to hold the strings of the national purse. Hence, corruption has impacted the allotment of resources to those rural communities where they are most needed.

Socially, the structure of the country is hierarchical, where those who hold power or are wealthy in society tend to be accorded enormous respect. In Ghana, the elderly as well as those in authority are highly respected, and most citizens who fall within this category are men. Unfortunately, in the Ghanaian society's structure, women tend to be at the bottom of the totem pole as they are "neither seen nor heard." This standard continues despite the robust legislative and policies initiated by the government to enhance the well-being of women and ensure that women are equitably accorded their rights to education, politics, sustainable development, and reproductive health (Dzorgbo & Gyan, 2016).

These Ghanaian realities are significant to our research because, as we shall see below, social hierarchies, inequality, and widespread poverty combine to make mental health care very difficult to access for most Ghanaians suffering from mental illness.

STIGMA: DEFINITIONS AND PARAMETERS

Stigma is the single most prevalent and impactful barrier to accessing mental health support within the developing world (Avoke, 2002; Agbenyega, 2003; Baffoe, 2013; Gyamfi et al., 2018). Stigma refers to negative and prejudicial manners in which people are labeled and treated based upon personal qualities and/or circumstances within their societies (Agbenyega, 2003; Goffman, 1963). It functions as a sign of disgrace, dishonor, and separation from the community, and it is intended to discredit a person with the illness (Abdullah & Brown, 2011; Gyamfi et al., 2018). Stigma is most commonly associated with mental health concerns. It is prevalent worldwide and a significant public health concern at a global level (Mfoafo-M'Carthy & Sossou, 2017; Gyamfi et al., 2018). Many people diagnosed with mental illness experience multiple levels of oppression: first, due to their struggles with the illness symptomology; and second, due to the stereotype(s), discrimination, prejudices, and oppression resulting from the stigma that are widespread throughout many societies (Corrigan & Watson, 2002; Mfoafo-M'Carthy & Sossou, 2017). This might include social judgment, degradation, and/or devaluation of those formally diagnosed with mental illness or labeled as having a mental illness (Abdullah & Brown, 2011). Stigma could be based on a multitude of factors; this may include superstition, ignorance, lack of knowledge, lack of empathy, tradition or belief systems, and fear toward those perceived to be different (Avoke, 2002; Agbenyega, 2003; Baffoe, 2013; Brydges & Mkandawire, 2018). Stigma is characterized by shame, blame, secrecy, negative labeling, and discrimination, often resulting in stereotyping, fear, embarrassment, anger, status loss, and social isolation and exclusion (Avoke, 2002; Agbenyega, 2003; Goffman, 1963). Individuals diagnosed with mental illness are at greater risk of stigmatization, especially when they are considered to have limited social skills, an unusual physical appearance, and symptoms of the illness are evident (Abdullah & Brown, 2011).

Stigma is composed of stereotyping, prejudice, and discrimination, all of which have specific definitions. Stereotyping is a collectively agreed-upon judgment about a specific group, a quickly generated impression, and an expectation for those who are perceived to belong within the group (Corrigan & Watson, 2002). This might include, for example, the impression and expectation that all people with mental illness are abnormal, unpredictable, violent, and incapable of contributing to society. Reflecting fundamentally negative beliefs, stereotyping often leads to prejudice, which can be defined as a normative and often negative mindset intended to yield an emotional response toward a specific group (Corrigan & Watson, 2002; Abdullah & Brown, 2011). The expectation that all people with mental illness are abnormal, unpredictable, and incapable may, for example, lead the community to feel discomfort and fear toward stigmatized individuals. In this case, prejudice often leads to discrimination, which the literature defines as unjust treatment, intentional and/or unintentional, of the stigmatized group based on stereotype(s) and prejudice (Corrigan &Watson, 2002; Goreczny et al., 2011). Discrimination fueled by stereotyping and prejudice produces harmful results, including avoidance of persons with mental illness, social, economic, and political exclusion, and the refusal to provide mental health support within the community (Abdullah & Brown, 2011; Corrigan & Watson, 2002). Discrimination, which can be both obvious and subtle, may also lead to exclusion, bullying, aggression and violence, ridicule, and devaluation of the stigmatized group. In many cases, this encourages the oppression of persons with mental illness and significantly impacts their ability to obtain housing, maintain consistent employment, access education, receive treatment and support, and experience an adequate quality of life (Abdullah & Brown, 2011; Baffoe, 2013).

Stigma can be public or self-imposed by individuals who are part of the stigmatized group. Public stigma is the reaction, or discriminatory response, of the general population toward those who are perceived to belong to a stigmatized group (Abdullah & Brown, 2011; Corrigan & Watson, 2002). It often results in discrimination, which is evident when a person or system—such as the government, criminal justice system, or healthcare system—does not place value on the stigmatized group and, due to prejudice, engages in behavior that has a negative impact on this group (or purposively disengages from behaviors that might be positive). For example, to cite just one common scenario, an employer who does not believe that people with mental illness are competent might refuse to employ them (Abdullah & Brown, 2011). This kind of discrimination, fueled by public stigma, can have a significant negative impact on stigmatized individuals and often leads to self-stigmatization, questioning their own capabilities and worth. Self-stigma, in other words, develops when an individual internalizes negative public perceptions and prejudices (Abdullah & Brown, 2011; Corrigan & Watson, 2002). It is often characterized by shame, demoralization, decreased self-esteem, and diminished self-efficacy (Baffoe, 2013). This may encourage an individual to believe that they are less appreciated and respected within society based simply on their membership of a publicly stigmatized group.

Self-stigma, in turn, potentially leads individuals to engage in detrimental or self-sabotaging behavior. One example would be an individual with mental illness who does not include a cover letter with a job application, despite an explicit requirement to do so, because of their belief that they will not seriously be considered for the position. This not only guarantees that they will lose the job opportunity, but it also can, and often does, result in a self-fulfilling prophecy where, because the self-sabotaging behavior produces a negative outcome, the initial reason for the sabotage is confirmed. The underlying stereotype and consequent action are thereby enforced (Abdullah & Brown, 2011). This cycle is extremely prevalent and debilitating for those within stigmatized groups.

DISABILITY STIGMA IN AFRICA AND GHANA

What do we know from the existing literature about stigma toward disability in Ghana? To move beyond stereotypes and popular media impressions of the widespread persecution of Ghanaians with disabilities, we must begin with a systematic definition of stigma. We define stigma in terms of attitudes and stereotypes that discredit individuals and groups, portraying them as inferior as measured against social "norms" defined by members of society without disability (Ahmedani, 2011; Goffman, 1963; Dudley, 2000). Following this definition, recent research has uncovered widespread stigma toward disability across the African continent, including mental illness and physical disabilities. Regarding the former, researchers have found unexpectedly high levels of stigma toward persons with mental illnesses among Nigerian clergy and university students, toward persons with psychotic illnesses in South Africa, and in primary schools in Kenya (Adewuya & Makanjuola, 2005; Egbe, 2015; Igbinomwanhia & Omoaregba, 2013; Ndetei et al., 2016). Persons with physical disabilities also experience stigma across the African continent, as evidenced by our recent collection that gathered scholars based in Africa to report on their country's experiences with the United Nations Convention on the Rights of Persons with Disabilities. The contributors reported widespread stigma and discrimination at the community level and even by family members and loved ones. In cases as diverse as Ethiopia, Cameroon, Uganda, Zimbabwe, and South Africa, persons with physical disabilities are denied personhood and stripped of agency over decision-making. Stigma also means that many governments hesitate to support disability programs (Grischow & Mfoafo-M'Carthy, 2022).

In Ghana specifically, persons with disabilities are reportedly among the country's most excluded members of society (Geurts & Komabu-Pompeyie, 2013). High levels of stigma exist toward mental illness within families, in public settings and workplaces, and even among health service providers. For example, one study found that many families deserted loved ones who had been diagnosed with mental illnesses, and community members harassed and molested them or accused them of being witches (Dako-Gyeke & Asumang, 2013). Another study of three Ghanaian psychiatric hospitals reported widespread stigma rooted in their family's fears that mental illness produced unpredictable and potentially violent behaviors (Barke et al., 2011). Further studies echo these findings and emphasize the harmful effects of stigma toward mental illness, including social isolation and the denial of food and the basic necessities of life to relatives with mental disorders (Tawiah, 2012; Thornicroft et al., 2007). Ghanaians with mental illness are also stigmatized and discriminated against in the workplace, either by being denied employment or dismissed after receiving a diagnosis (Barke et al., 2011; Dako-Gyeke & Asumang, 2013).

Similar experiences of stigma have been found among Ghanaians with physical disabilities. Existing research shows that stigma toward physical disability is a significant problem in Ghana (Mprah, 2022; Naami, 2022). In many cases, persons with disabilities are denied humanity and personhood (Moasun, 2019) or at best considered incapable of performing productive work (Reynolds, 2010). Stigma in this form has serious consequences, including personal harm and the denial of rights in healthcare, employment, politics, and/or public life (Amosun et al., 2013; Kassah, 2012; Sarfo et al., 2017). Denied biomedical healthcare, many Ghanaians with disabilities turn to herbalists for treatment (Amosun et al., 2013; Sarfo et al., 2017). In the economic sphere, Ghanaians with disabilities have trouble finding and keeping jobs, leading to higher underemployment and unemployment, lower incomes, and more poverty than Ghanaians without disabilities (Mensah et al., 2015; Sackey, 2015). Unemployment and poverty also limit their participation in public life, as few have the means to participate, and those who secure political positions face discrimination and find it difficult to carry out their responsibilities (Sackey, 2015).

As with mental illness, stigma toward physical disability in Ghana is often rooted in spiritual beliefs—both traditional and Christian—that associate disability with evil, magical powers, sorcery, and witchcraft, which are connected to both traditional beliefs and Christianity (Kassah, 2008). Notable studies have reported the belief that children with disabilities are supernatural punishments for wrongs committed by their parents (Botts & Evans, 2011; Kassah, 2008; Naami & Heyashi, 2012; Reynolds, 2010; Sackey, 2015). In other cases, children with disabilities themselves are believed to be non-human, either traditional bush or river spirits (Denham et al., 2010) or demons or devils in a Christian sense (Kassah, 2014). In sum, the literature shows that Ghanaians with physical disabilities are often considered "subnormal" humans who cannot have proper social roles and, therefore, are excluded from social, economic, and political participation (Ganle et al., 2016; Kassah et al., 2012, 2014).

RESEARCH METHODOLOGY

This book has arisen from two projects on disability in Ghana, both funded by the Social Sciences Research and Humanities Council of Canada (SSHRC). The first was a two-year program on stigma and disability, with a major focus on psychosocial disabilities, carried out between 2017 and 2019. The second was a five-year program on the history and lived experience of disability rights, which also began in 2017. Over the course of the projects, we conducted fieldwork with many participants: 120 for the psychosocial disability project and 300 for the oral history project. In both cases, we developed semi-structured questionnaires that included questions about the participants' lived experience with stigma. The fieldwork focused on the experience of stigma as well as its impact in the areas of social inclusion and exclusion, psychological well-being and personhood, employment, and political participation. We designed the project in a way that privileges the voices of Ghanaians with disabilities. We take an approach similar to Participatory Action Research (PAR), in which researchers work in partnership with local communities to carry out fieldwork anchored in the direct experience of participants (Baum et al., 2006).

To recruit participants, the research team used a combination of purposive and snowball sampling, targeting Ghanaians with psychosocial and physical disabilities. Under purposive sampling, researchers intentionally select specific populations as a pool from which to draw participants (Patton 2002). Our research obviously required this approach due to its focus on persons with disabilities. We worked with Ghanaian partners to target disabled participants who were able to express their experiences fully, either in English or a local Ghanaian language. Further recruiting, where necessary, was done by snowball sampling via word-of-mouth. For participants with mental illness, our inclusion criteria included a formal diagnosis and a four-month minimum hospital stay (past or present), as well as the patients' ability to exhibit insights into their conditions and express themselves clearly enough for us to understand their insights. Caregivers had to be actively engaged in taking care of a family member and willing to speak freely about their experiences. For participants with physical disabilities, we recruited as broadly as possible in collaboration with Ghanaian disability scholars with whom we have worked since 2018. Ethics for the study were approved by the Wilfrid Laurier University (WLU) Research Ethics Board. In the field, researchers and their assistants spent time in these communities, meeting with them and getting to know them before embarking on this study. Participants met with a researcher for a period of between half an hour and an hour plus to answer questions on their experiences and challenges with regard to stigma and discrimination.

The interviews were based on semi-structured questionnaires that standardized responses but allowed the participants to expand on their comments. The interviews addressed four main research questions: (1) What are the main experiences of stigma in the lives of persons with mental illness and physical disability in Ghana? (2) What are the roots of disability stigma in Ghana? (3) What are the consequences of disability stigma in Ghana? (4) What are the public policy implications of this research?

Our data analysis strategies followed Braun and Clarke (2006) and Creswell (2013). First, we familiarized ourselves with the data by transcribing the interviews, reading them in detail several times, making brief notes, and dividing the stories into small thematic segments. Second, we followed Creswell's model of "lean coding," using NVivo software to create a short list of tentative codes aligning with the data segments—an approach also recommended by Braun and Clarke for generating initial codes. We then expanded the codes into a final list, reading and re-reading the transcripts, and continuing to code and analyze the data until no new themes or categories emerged. Following Braun and Clarke, we used the codes to generate potential themes and checked to ensure that the themes reflected the codes and the data set. Finally, as Creswell recommends, we produced a list of themes and subthemes across the participants' responses. Discussions between the researchers resolved contradictions and inconsistencies in the terms and themes. Using Silverman (2015) as a guide, we also took several steps to ensure the reliability and validity of our data. For maximum reliability, a study's findings should be replicable and independent of outside influences connected to the interview process. To achieve reliability, we had multiple researchers double-check the transcriptions and data analysis. To ensure validity, which refers to the accurate representation of data, we interviewed enough participants to reach saturation (i.e., until clear common themes had emerged), and we compared narratives across different interview times and locations. We further strengthened our data's validity by using an inductive approach to analysis, letting the stories speak for themselves, and we present the stories below in the participants' own words as much as possible.

Interviews for this project were audio-recorded, transcribed, and edited for grammatical errors. A content analysis approach was used to analyze the data gathered. In doing this, all transcripts were read through thoroughly and guided by the stated objectives of the study; codes that carried some levels of meaning reminiscent of the objectives of the study were identified and highlighted. The transcripts were read through a second time, where codes were organized into categories in a similar manner. These categories were further grouped into themes. Like themes were then grouped and labeled, producing overarching themes with a number of subthemes. Upon developing overarching and subthemes, evidence in the form of voice quotes from the transcripts of participants was selected from the statements where initial codes were developed. Protecting the participants' anonymity was very important—especially in the case of Ghanaians diagnosed with mental illness. Therefore, we have not used actual names, and we have not linked specific caregivers to the patients. Instead, we assigned pseudonyms to all quotations in compliance with the ethical principles of confidentiality and anonymity.

OUTLINE OF THE BOOK

The book is presented in three parts. Part I establishes the context for our analysis, including this introductory chapter as well as chapter 1, which surveys the history of disability in Ghana from the precolonial period to the present. It is very difficult to reconstruct the history of disability in Ghana before the colonial period; indeed, even before the 1940s, we feel that it is important to attempt to root out that history from the materials that are available. These include oral traditions such as epic poetry and proverbs, as well as the accounts of early European travelers. While very thin, these sources nonetheless offer some insights into the experience of physical disability, deafness, and blindness; they also provide clues about precolonial explanations of disability. Regarding the latter, there is evidence that precolonial African societies ascribed disability to spiritual causes, although it must be said that this was common practice in Europe at this time as well. The precolonial record also indicates a variety of responses to disability, including stigmatization and acceptance. As we shall discover, this is true for Africa generally as well as present-day Ghana, as reflected in the proverbs of the Akan ethnic group. Where precolonial African societies accepted persons with disabilities, it can be inferred that families and communities looked after their needs, and certainly there was not the modern expectation that persons with disabilities should be rehabilitated to contribute "productively to society." Moving on to the colonial period, chapter 2 highlights a shift in the perception and approach to disability, in which the colonial administration of Ghana moved toward a rehabilitation approach premised on the idea that persons with disabilities had to be "normalized and integrated into their communities as "productive" members of society. This is significant, because it continues to impact the experiences of persons with disabilities in Ghana today.

Part II presents the findings of our field work in Ghana, focusing on the experience of stigma as reported by Ghanaians with disabilities and their caregivers. Chapter 3 focuses on the cultural roots of stigma, broadly defined to include language and indigenous beliefs. Drawing on interviews conducted across Ghana, the chapter begins by analyzing language as a cultural tool in relation to perceptions of disability. Most importantly, the analysis emphasizes the role of language in producing cultural identity and the concomitant manner in which cultural identity impacts the ways in which people relate to each other in any given society. The testimonies show that language plays an important role in creating Canadian cultural identities that stigmatize disability. This conclusion leads into an analysis of indigenous beliefs about disability that are shaped by language and reinforce stigma and its negative consequences. These beliefs include the idea presented in the introduction that persons with disabilities are considered non-human and not worthy of social inclusion. The chapter finishes with a discussion of stereotypes and myths about disability in Ghana that arise from cultural norms and beliefs. The widespread prevalence of stereotypes and myths is shown clearly in the narratives that are analyzed in this chapter.

Chapter 4 extends the cultural analysis to shine a light more specifically on religion and spirituality in connection to stigma toward Ghanaians with mental illness. This is a very important topic in Ghana because persons with mental illness are among the most stigmatized and excluded members of Ghanaian society. The chapter argues that perceptions of mental illness and its causes are deeply rooted in religion and spiritual beliefs among the Ghanaian populace. The analysis builds upon the observation presented in the introduction that negative attitudes toward mental illness in Ghana stem largely from beliefs in spiritual causes. Interestingly, the belief that mental illness is caused by spiritual forces such as witchcraft is not only held by Ghanaians without disabilities, but it has also been internalized by many persons with disabilities. At the same time, however, non-African religions (mainly Islam and Christianity) also provide people diagnosed with mental illness with a sense of refuge. Also, organized religion can provide support and coping mechanisms through mosques and churches. The chapter concludes by calling for collaboration between biomedical psychiatric professionals and faith-based healers, both traditional and Muslim or Christian. Ghana will remain a highly spiritual and religious country, making it necessary to incorporate spirituality into programs for mental health in the future.

Chapter 5 shifts the analysis to the daily lived experience of disability stigma on persons with disabilities (including mental illness and physical disabilities). The chapter surveys the literature on stigma toward disability globally and in Ghana. Moving beyond spiritual beliefs about the causes of disability, we present the actual causes of disability as reported by our respondents, including accidents, illnesses, and harmful medical interventions. The chapter then surveys the experience and impact of stigma among Ghanaians with disabilities. The latter includes negative labeling, the denial of the right to marry, psychological suffering through stereotypes, the experience of disrespect, abuse, and social exclusion. The chapter concludes with a call for a collective effort by the Ghanaian government, NGOs, and other civil society organizations to combat stigma toward persons with disabilities. Chapter 6 provides a unique analysis of disability stigma and its impact on caregivers as well as persons with disabilities. The conclusion summarizes the main points of each chapter and highlights their significance for improving disability policy and programs in Ghana.

NOTE

1. In Ghana, the most notable PWD to succeed on the world stage is the disabled athlete Emmanuel Yeboah, whose determination and success led to a film narrated by Oprah Winfrey and a children's book (Thompson and Qualls 2015). We have worked with others who are lesser known but equally important, including Peter Obeng Asamoa (Executive Director of the Ghana Blind Union), Gertrude Fefoame (Chair of the United Nations Committee on the Rights of Persons with Disabilities), and Dr. Henry Siedu Daanaa, a lawyer with a vision disability who served as Ghana's Minister for Chieftaincy and Culture between 2013 and 2017.

Chapter 1

The History of Disability in Ghana

INTRODUCTION

Historical contexts are very important to the understanding of the experience of disability in the contemporary world. Historicizing disability helps us to understand the ways in which past attitudes and practices are embedded within current experiences of stigma, discrimination, and resilience. It also helps us to identify shifts and changes in approaches to disability, including programs and policies, which can be useful in designing future interventions. In the case of disability in Ghana—as well as in Africa generally—investigating history reveals that traditional attitudes and behaviors toward persons with disabilities still exist, but that they have been overlaid with new assumptions connected to European colonialism. As we shall discover below, there are significant challenges in rooting out this history, but it is an important exercise.

Over the past thirty years, a "New History of Disability" has arisen that has produced a relatively large body of literature on the historical experiences of persons with disabilities. Emerging out of Western disability rights movements in the 1970s, it produced revisionist work treating persons with disabilities as agents of their own histories and not merely objects of charity (Barton & Oliver, 1997; Longmore & Umansky, 2001). This approach has led to calls for research into historical experiences from the perspective of actors with disabilities (Kudlick, 2003), as well as research focused on blindness (Barasch, 2001; Ferguson, 2001), deafness (Burch, 2002; Branson & Miller, 2002; Buchanan, 2002), rehabilitation (Borsay, 2006; Bunzel, 2007), and the experiences of war veterans with disabilities (Anderson, 2011; Cohen, 2001; Gerber, 2012). However, these studies have focused largely on Western societies and the experience of disability under industrial capitalism

(Longmore & Umansky, 2001). Disability history in the Global South, much less Africa, is still in its infancy, and the few studies that exist tend to focus on the colonial period and after.

For Africa, Julie Livingston's research on disability in Botswana remains the seminal contribution to the field (Livingston, 2005, 2006). Grischow (2011a, 2011b, 2015) has produced work on colonial and postcolonial disability policies and experiences in Ghana, and there are good studies of asylums in Nigeria (Sadowsky, 1999) and attitudes toward disability in Ethiopia (Teklemariam, 2010). Driedger's history of international disability rights briefly mentions Zimbabwe and French West Africa (Driedger, 1989), and some research has explored Southern Africa after 1980 (Charlton, 1993; Howell et al., 2006; Malinga, 1999; Miles, 1996). Iliffe's study of poverty in Africa contains a brief discussion of disability in the 1940s and 1950s (Iliffe, 1987). Most recently, Gebrekidan's survey of disability rights activism in Kenya covers the late colonial period but stops at 1961 (Gebrekidan, 2012). Still, Gebrekidan's work is seminal because of its use of nontraditional written sources, including newspapers, memoirs, and the archived papers of Kenyan Disabled People's Organization (DPOs). For precolonial Africa, the only studies we have found are Miles' surveys (Miles, 2004, n.d.)—many of which remain unpublished—and Scalenghe's analysis of the history of disability in the Ottoman Empire, which includes material on North Africa (Scalenghe, 2014, 2018).

Mindful of the challenges in reconstructing the history of disability in Africa and Ghana, this chapter offers a survey of the precolonial and colonial periods. Two main insights arise from the analysis. First, in the precolonial era, we can find evidence of stigma and discrimination toward persons with disabilities, but also acceptance and social inclusion. Regarding the latter, precolonial African social systems offered support networks and practices for all extended family members, including individuals with disabilities. However, oral traditions, including epic poems and proverbs, indicate that mistreatment also existed. Second, moving ahead to the colonial period, we can perceive a shift in attitudes toward disability in which European colonial officials (British in the case of Ghana) imposed the Western idea that persons with disabilities were inferior because they were considered nonproductive from the perspective of work. As such, they had to be "normalized" through rehabilitation in order to become integrated as full citizens, where citizenship was defined largely by one's capacity to work. This is an important finding because the Western idea of rehabilitation and the dignity of work persists today and operates as an important factor behind stigma and discrimination. The following discussion addresses these themes, beginning with the precolonial era and moving on to colonialism and independence in Ghana.

DISABILITY IN AFRICA DURING THE PRECOLONIAL PERIOD

It is very difficult to reconstruct the history of disability in precolonial Africa, let alone the territory that became Ghana. Written sources are limited to Muslim chronicles beginning in the thirteenth century and European travelers' accounts in the 1700s and 1800s. The former contains very little, if any, information about disability or blindness, while the information in the European accounts is very minimal and scattered throughout multiple publications. Beyond these sources, there also exist oral traditions and proverbs that can be mined for some information about the history of disability. In some cases, this material can be accessed in written form, but researchers also must rely on the accounts of contemporary fieldwork participants who are familiar with traditions surrounding disability. Putting these sources together, it is possible to reconstruct some aspects of the history of disability and blindness in Ghana, although it is necessary to widen the scope to Africa generally in order to produce a more thorough picture of attitudes and practices in the region generally.

As we shall discover, two main points can be gleaned from the available sources on disability history in Africa during the precolonial era. First, as was the case in premodern Europe and other global regions, the causes of disability were believed to lie in the spiritual realm. Second, there is some evidence of social acceptance of certain disabilities, particularly blindness, and even cultural practices putting them in positions of power, but there are also instances of stigma and social exclusion.

Evidence of physical disability, deafness, and blindness in Africa can be found in the historical record.[1] One of the earliest written sources containing evidence of physical disability in Africa is an epic poem written about Sundiata Keita, the first ruler of the Empire of Mali (to the north of present-day Ghana) from 1235 to 1255. Most versions of the poem, as well as other commentaries that have been handed down over the generations, describe Sundiata as being unable to walk as a boy and young man. The descriptions differ between sources. One of the most well-known states that around the age of twelve, "Sunjata could not crawl, much less stand up, much less walk," while another says that he could only crawl for the first seven years of his life. None of the traditional accounts of Sundiata attempt to explain his disability, but they do point to a remedy in the form of an iron prosthetic. One advisor is said to have suggested that they "forge iron and give it to him so that he may rise up" (Suso & Kanute, 2006, p. 61), after which "they quarried iron ore and smelted it, and they fashioned it into a very long rod. They cut it in two and they bent it. Three full-grown men took each rod and brought it" (Suso & Kanute, 2006, pp. ix, 13, 61–63, 80, 112, 115, 116).

Regarding deafness, some early European travelers' in West Africa encountered deaf persons and commented on proverbs about deafness and the use of local sign languages. However, the information is very thin, and, especially with respect to sign language, it is unclear whether it was necessarily connected to deafness. Regarding the latter, William Towerson's account of his visit to the coast in the 1550s reported that he and the English traders communicated with African leaders and traders through signing, but the signs appear to have been connected simply to trade between different language speakers, not deafness (Towerson, 1555–1556). However, a later explorer, Tremearne, reported the use of sign language among the Hausa of present-day Northern Nigeria. During his visit, Tremearne heard a Hausa story about someone who stole another's property and pretended to be deaf and mute in order to escape punishment. Tremearne quoted the story as follows:

> The King showed his hand to the Deaf-Mute in the manner that one questions a Deaf-Mute [i.e., by the sign-language], and the Man replied (on his hands) that the property was his. Then one of the Councillors rose up and said "O King, see what the Deaf-Mute is doing, he is abusing you." The thief called out that this was not so, and by speaking betrayed his trick, and so he lost the case. (Tremearne, 1913, p. 49)

For our purposes, the significance of the story lies in the fact that local sign language was being used in Hausaland in the precolonial period. Tremearne actually presented a list of Hausa sign language gestures later in the book (pp. 56–57). But he also reported evidence of stigma and ill treatment of deaf-mute persons—for example, in the description of the Hausa word for deaf-mute, writing that "He or she sits alone, with tears streaming down the cheeks, or runs around, mouthing, in either case making no sound" (Tremearne, 1913, p. 536).

Turning to perceived causes of disability, the little evidence we have suggests that precolonial African societies attributed disability to spiritual causes. For instance, a Hausa legend recorded by Tremearne presents the story "about a woman who had never given birth, and at last she said 'O God, wilt Thou not give me even a Cripple or a Leper to bring forth?' And lo, God caused her to conceive, and she brought forth a Son (with a physical disability), and called him Little Crab" (Tremearne, 1913, p. 351). The mother asked a traditional priest to cure the disability so that the boy could walk. The priest agreed. However, believing the child was not human but a "Water-Spirit," the priest abandoned him at a riverbank to return him to the water where he belonged (Tremearne, 1913, p. 351).

Finding evidence of precolonial attitudes or actions toward disability in Ghana or elsewhere in Africa is very difficult, and few attempts have been made by scholars to investigate this topic. One exception is the scholar-activist M. Miles, who has attempted to piece together precolonial disability history in Africa. In several publications and personal papers, Miles searched for evidence of attitudes and experiences of persons with deafness, blindness, and (to a lesser extent) physical disability in the areas of archaeology, folklore, and first-hand accounts of economic activities and connections to precolonial Royal Courts. In relation to physical disability, Miles found evidence of both stigmatization and acceptance of persons with disabilities. The Hausa legend quoted above implies stigmatization, in that, first, the birth of a child with a disability happened out of the mother's desperation; second, the mother felt the need to "fix," the child; and, third, the traditional priest discarded the boy in the belief that he was a Water-Spirit and not human.

Miles also found evidence of stigmatization of deaf persons in sources as diverse as Egyptian hieroglyphs, Ethiopian and Ugandan folk tales, and European accounts of Nigerian cultural practices. In the latter case, Europeans encountered cases of deaf persons being ostracized by chiefs and elders in northern Nigeria and even traded across the continent to the Ottoman Empire, whose rulers had a tradition of employing death attendants (Miles, 2004). However, despite this stigma toward deafness, some early European travelers among the Hausa also discovered the existence of a standardized sign language used by deaf persons to communicate with others in urban centers such as Kano (Miles, n.d.). But on the whole, the admittedly scant record indicates that stigma toward deafness was common across the African continent. Interestingly, one of the exceptions was found in Ghana. Turning to Ghana, there is one very important example of a deaf community being founded in the 1700s and developing into a deaf-majority village called Adamorobe (Miles, 2004). Turning to blindness, the historical record suggests relatively more social acceptance and inclusion, at least in some areas where written sources exist. For example, the city of Kano in present-day Northern Nigeria had a community of blind persons, complete with their own chief, with origins perhaps dating as far back as the 1200s (Miles, n.d.; Palmer, 1928).

Turning to Ghana, the absence of written evidence makes it very difficult to assess precolonial attitudes toward disability. However, Ghanaian proverbs can provide a useful proxy. The works of Moasun and Mfoafo-M'Carthy (Moasun, 2019; Moasun & Mfoafo-M'Carthy, 2021) has surveyed 7,000 Akan proverbs collected by Appiah and Appiah (2007) and found seventy-five that related to disability. While none of the proverbs refer to deafness or blindness, many relate to physical disabilities, and some focus on mental illness. Echoing the examples collected by Miles, most of the Akan proverbs reveal stigma toward disability, but some also point to social acceptance. On stigma, one proverb implies that Akan communities ostracized mothers of children born with disabilities: "*Obi mma bafan ni due da* [One never commiserates with a disabled [*sic*] child's mother]." Many researchers would attribute this sentiment to the traditional belief that children with disabilities were born because their mothers were spiritually cursed (Moasun & Mfoafo-M'Carthy, 2021, p. 920). In any case, the proverb clearly presents disability as a negative and cautions community members not to draw attention to the mothers.

Moving to a specific disability, the Akan proverbs presented by Appiah and Appiah convey a definite sense of stigma toward persons with angular kyphosis. For instance, one proverb states that "*Yɛde hia na ɛware akyakya.* [Poverty makes us marry a hunchback]." The clear implication here is that a poor person who cannot afford a regular dowry will be forced to marry a person with low social status, such as an individual with angular kyphosis (p. 921). This stigma is reinforced in another proverb:

> *Sɛ wɔpamo akyakyani na woanto no a, na ɛnyɛ ne mmirika-tuo ntira na mmom ne ho sereɛ ntira.* [If you chase a hunchback and you don't succeed, it is not because of his swiftness but because of his laughable figure.]

Interestingly, Appiah and Appiah (2007, p. 242) interpret this in a positive light, arguing that it means that "some apparent disadvantages bring advantages." However, it seems more likely to present the message that persons with angular kyphosis deserve to be mocked (Moasun & Mfoafo-M'Carthy, 2021, p. 921).

Other proverbs about physical disability present a more complicated picture. One very interesting example is the following: "*Ɔnim abɔnsamu* [If a (person with a disability of the legs) does not know anything else, he knows how to clap his hands]." This can be read negatively in that the individual can only perform a limited function. However, one might read this saying more positively if it is taken as a metaphor for persons with disabilities having other abilities—perhaps being "differently abled." Another proverb very interestingly points to the use of prosthetics in precolonial Akan societies, similar to the case of Sundiata: "*Obi rennya sɛ dwumfoɔ awo bafan* [No one is as fortunate as the blacksmith who gives birth to child with impairments in the legs]." Not only does this say that disability can be a boon for blacksmiths, it also implies that families offered prosthetics to help children with physical disabilities to integrate into their communities. Two final Akan proverbs are even more interesting with respect to physical disabilities:

> *Abasini twe adeɛ bɔn mu na amma a, na emfiri ne nsa, na mmom biribi ntira.* [If a person with one arm amputated pulls something from a hole and it does not come, then it is not because of his arm but because of something else.]

This saying points to the belief that persons with disabilities are not necessarily incapable of performing the same activities as their counterparts without disabilities. The idea that one-armed persons were not always stigmatized is also conveyed in a proverb connected to the story of an Akan king: "*Obiri nti na yɛnum basini nsa* [It is because of Obiri that we drink the drink of the one-armed man]."

As discussed by Moasun and Mfoafo-M'Carthy (2021), Nana Obiri Yeboa, who ruled the Asante Kingdom of Ghana from 1660 to 1680, reportedly employed a personal palm-wine tapper with a disability (he was missing an arm and he was infected). However, out of respect for Nana Obiri Yeboa, the people still drank his wine. It is difficult, if not impossible, to read community attitudes into this proverb. One might equally interpret this as indicating stigma (as in "we are not happy drinking wine from the one-armed man") or as acceptance ("the king accepts the one-armed man, so we should, too"). In any case, what is most interesting is the fact that the proverb offers evidence to support the story that Nana Ofori Yeboa employed a wine-tapper with a disability, which suggests that disability perhaps was not universally stigmatized in Akan societies and that, in some cases, persons with physical disabilities were actively included in community activities (Moasun & Mfoafo-M'Carthy, 2021).

Regarding mental illness, two proverbs imply that mental illness was stigmatized in precolonial Akan societies:

> *Ɔbɔdamfoɔ na odidi sumina soɔ.* [It is the madman [*sic*] who eats on the rubbish heap.]

> *Ɔbɔdamfoɔ se ne dam kɔ a, na nyɛ deɛ Ode hunahuna mmɔfra.* [If a madman says his madness is gone, a little remains for frightening children.]

Two further proverbs related to Akan society's treatment of persons with mental illness, advising communities to forcibly confine them to eliminate the threat and return the communities to stability:

> *Ɔbaakofoɔ nkyere bɔdamfoɔ.* [One person does not arrest a lunatic.]

> *ƆbɔdamfoO a yɛato no dawɛmfoɔ na ɔka n'asɛm sɛ "dawɛmfoɔ adaworoma na ama amanfoɔ ahyɛ me nso."* [A madman [*sic*] who is kept in shackles told his tale thus: "Thanks to the shackles, I am recognized by all the people in the state."]

These proverbs imply that persons with mental illness are too dangerous to be confined by a single person—this requires a group—and that only when they are shackled are persons with mental illness deemed safe for their communities.

A final theme arising from the limited record of disability in precolonial Africa concerns family and community treatment of persons with disabilities. Despite the existence of stigma, we know from evidence dating to the 1600s that social systems had developed in Africa on the basis of kinship and extended family support for all members of families and communities, including persons with disabilities. Family and community care for persons with disabilities developed from an early date in Christian Northeast Africa and Muslim West Africa. Similar provisions existed in Botswana, where individuals with disabilities "were considered full members of society, complete with all the responsibilities prescribed by gender, status and age" (Miles, n.d.). Across precolonial Africa, there is little evidence that disability was considered something to be mitigated through rehabilitation, in order to integrate Africans with disabilities into supposedly "normal" society.

DISABILITY IN COLONIAL GHANA

The formal colonization of Ghana dates to 1874–1902, when Britain created the colony of the Gold Coast (in present-day southern Ghana) in 1874 and added the Protectorates of Ashanti and the Northern Territories in 1901–1902. Although disability surely existed in the colony, there is almost no evidence of attitudes or practices toward persons with disabilities before the 1930s. At this time, the first disability programs were church-based and focused on education for children with visual impairments. The earliest reference we have found is from 1936, when a Scottish Missionary named Reverend Harker founded a school for blind children—initially serving only two students—in Akropong Akwapi (Mamah et al., 2011). This was followed in 1947 by another Presbyterian school for visually impaired children in Begoro, Eastern Region (Obeng, 2007). In the meantime, between 1944 and 1947, the colonial administration attempted to develop a rehabilitation center in Accra for West African soldiers disabled from war injuries. Focusing on acquired physical disabilities (but not war-blinded soldiers, who were sent to Nigeria), the center sought to reintegrate the ex-soldiers into the regular workforce or provide work in sheltered workshops. Initially developed for soldiers from the Gold Coast Regiment of the West African Frontier Force in mid-1945, the Colonial Office expanded its mandate to soldiers from the other British West African colonies (Nigeria, the Gambia, and Sierra Leone) as well as civilians. Although several hundred patients came through the center in 1944–1945, after 1945 the numbers dropped significantly, and the center was closed in 1947 (Grischow, 2011).

Despite this failure, discussions about African disability at the Colonial Office produced a follow-up visit to British colonies in Africa (including the Gold Coast), the Middle East, and Asia to investigate the prevalence and causes of blindness. John Wilson led the team and its report on colonial blindness in 1948 had a significant influence on disability initiatives in Ghana (Ridley, 1945). Wilson's report recommended abandoning the West African regional center at Lagos (part of the colonial plan in the 1940s) in favor of local programs in each colony focused on civilians rather than veterans. To this end, Wilson created the British Empire Society for the Blind (BESB) in 1950 as a charitable organization with Colonial Office support. During the 1950s, the BESB opened branches across West Africa (WA), including twenty-seven on the Gold Coast alone by 1952 (Great Britain, 1948; Iliffe, 1988; Wilson, 1963).

DISABILITY IN INDEPENDENT GHANA I: EDUCATION, WELFARE, AND CHARITY, 1950S1970S

The BESB's branches were joined in the late 1950s by other new disability institutions. In 1957, an African American pastor, Reverend Andrew Foster, opened a school for the deaf in Accra. In 1958, the Methodist opened a school for children with visual impairments in WA and a school for persons with physical disabilities (Mamah et al., 2011; Obeng, 2007). In late 1960, Sir John Wilson returned to Ghana to undertake a survey of disability (Grischow, 2011b). The final report recommended a national program of rehabilitation for Ghanaian adults with disabilities and special education programs for children with disabilities, as well as integrated training and education programs for skills development (Government of Ghana, 1961). Specific recommendations included a national network of urban and rural rehabilitation units and the development of special education programs in Ghana's public schools. Wilson also argued for centralized government control over the rehabilitation units, supplemented by private voluntary associations. The program would be preceded by a registration drive undertaken by the Department of Social Welfare and Community Development.

Based on Wilson's recommendations, the Convention People's Party (CPP) developed a program of registration and rehabilitation beginning in 1961, which registered 13,608 Ghanaians with disabilities by 1964 (Adoo, 1964). While the registration campaign unfolded, the CPP opened the first rehabilitation center—the "Industrial Rehabilitation Unit"—in Accra in February 1963, which offered training in carpentry, metal working, and farm gardening (Adoo, 1963). This was followed by eight Rural Rehabilitation Units, offering instruction in farming, poultry raising, house construction, tailoring, sandal-making, and "one or more rural crafts" (Government of Ghana, 1964,

p. 20). Initially confined to men, Ghana's rehabilitation program expanded its services to women in 1964, in a program led by a colleague of John Wilson's, named Grace Ingham. The program included training for productive work to allow the attendees to integrate into the national workforce, and Ingham also sent some of the women to the rehabilitation units to train alongside their male counterparts (Ingham, 1964; Wilson, 1963).

In addition to rehabilitation, Nkrumah's government also developed a special education program based on John Wilson's recommendations. In 1961, the CPP's National Education Act mandated the government to take over the education of children with disabilities (Anthony, 2009). Where possible, except in cases of severe disabilities, the Act called on educators to integrate students with disabilities into the mainstream school system. Only in severe cases were students to be sent to segregated special schools (Obeng, 2007). The CPP followed this up with the Special Education Policy Act of 1962, which reinforced the policy of integrating students with disabilities, where possible, into mainstream schools. "The policy is very strong on integration," writes Obeng, stating that "pupils with physical disabilities are educated in the mainstream and that a wide range of support be made available to the regular school—classrooms assistance at preschool level, additional pedagogical support and periodic access to visiting specialists." Furthermore, Obeng also observes, "whereas children with severe learning difficulties attend mainstream schools but also get special classes in addition, those with only hearing and/or visual impairment attend regular or mainstream class but have support teaching in such classes" (Obeng, 2007, p. 97).

The CPP's rehabilitation and special education policies can be criticized for being controlled tightly by Nkrumah's government (which they were) and focusing too heavily on transforming "unproductive" Ghanaians with disabilities into productive workers in Ghana's national workforce. However, Nkrumah's disability programs also laid the foundation for the development of grassroots DPOs during the 1960s, developed and controlled by Ghanaians with disabilities (Guerts, personal communication). During this period, a generation of Ghanaians with vision disabilities led the way, many of whom had graduated from the mission schools created in the 1940s and "were beginning to reject practices of pity and charity and organized instead around principles of self-determination" (Geurts, 2015). Out of this group emerged the Ghana Association of the Blind (GAB), founded on December 15, 1963, by Lawrence Ansong, Paul Dotse, and Ben Quaye. Kathryn Geurts reported on this moment in an interview with Ansong, included in her path-breaking article on the history of the Accra Rehabilitation Center:

> "Blind persons' progress," Mr. Ansong said they called it back then. He had been a student in the sheltered workshop of The Centre, and when I interviewed

> him and asked about those early days, he emphatically said that GAB was different than GSB (Ghana Society for the Blind): "We did everything for ourselves; all officers were blind . . . it's an association OF, not FOR the blind. It's blind only. We do everything." (Guerts, 2015)

Other notable DPOs founded in Ghana during the 1960s included the Society of Friends of the Mentally Retarded Association (SFMRA), by parents of children with disabilities (Ntuli & Traore, 2013). In 1966, SFMRA lobbied successfully for the creation of Ghana's first "home for the mentally handicapped" (Ntuli & Traore, 2013, p. 50). Meanwhile, in 1961, Brother Tarcisius de Ruyter (SVD of the Divine Word Missionaries) founded an Orthopedic Training Centre and Mobile Orthopedic Unit in Nsawam, not far from Accra (OTC Ghana, n.d.).

During the 1970s, disability rights gained prominence globally with two UN declarations, one on developmental disabilities (1971) and one on disability in general (1975).[2] In 1976, the UN followed these declarations by announcing that 1981 would be the International Year of Disabled People (IYDP). These initiatives formed the backdrop for continued work on disability in Ghana, led by the Deputy Director of Rehabilitation, J.B. Amoako. Amoako had been trained in Great Britain and received substantial support from the West German government and the International Labor Organization (Burress, 1980). Under his leadership, the Rehabilitation Department collected data and produced regular reports on the state of disability services (Amoako, 1975). At this time, Ghanaians with disabilities were served by nine rehabilitation centers across the country, eight of which were rural (Walker, 1978). Additional services were provided by hospitals, the Labor Department, and the Ghana Education Service. In addition, in 1970, the home for developmentally challenged children started, and in 1966, it became the first "school for the mentally handicapped." This development anticipated a general trend toward the "rapid growth" in segregated schools for children with disabilities during the 1970s (Anthony, 2009; Avoke, 2001a).

DISABILITY IN INDEPENDENT GHANA II: FROM WELFARE TO DISABILITY RIGHTS, 1980–2008

During the 1980s, disability rights finally broke through as a major issue for the international community. Globally, the 1980 Rehabilitation International (RI) conference in Winnipeg, Canada, was a watershed moment for the international disability rights movement. Although RI was devoted entirely to disability issues, most of its board and membership were medical and social work professionals without disabilities. Fed up with the lack of representation by persons with disabilities, the delegates with disabilities presented a petition to RI demanding majority control over the organization. The RI rejected the petition, prompting the delegates with disabilities to decide to form their own organization, which they called, Disabled People's International (DPI). The founding conference was held in Singapore in 1981. At the conference, Vic Finkelstein and other members of the British Council of Organizations of Disabled People (BCDOP) lobbied the delegates to change the draft constitution's wording from the World Health Organization's (WHO) medical model to the social model.

After a heated discussion, the issue remained unresolved, resulting in tensions at DPI's birth between the British social model advocates and others (Driedger, 1989). Still, the RI and DPI conferences did have a lasting influence on the global disability rights movement, including Africa. First, they connected activists of persons with disabilities to each other and empowered them to create national disability organizations controlled by people with disabilities themselves. Second, the rise of the global disability movement pushed the UN to make good on several initiatives it had announced for the 1980s.

To prepare for the IYDP, in 1980 the UN sponsored a series of preparatory conferences held around the world, including regional meetings in Africa. This was followed by the World Program of Action Concerning Disabled Persons, released in 1982, and the International Decade of Disabled People from 1983–1992. During the International Decade, a series of African regional meetings produced reports on the status of persons with disabilities across the continent and issued recommendations for disability policies and programs (Economic Commission for Africa [ECA], 1980, 1987). Ghana participated in these meetings, and in the early 1980s, the Ghanaian government emerged as a leading light in African disability programs. As of March 1980, Ghana possessed

> the best organized, staffed and functioning system throughout the central sub-Sahara region providing rehabilitation services to more than 500 adults with disabilities annually. The program includes skilled well-trained staff counselors, trade instructors and supervisory personnel. The services include physical restoration, travel facility and skills, artificial limbs, wheelchairs, braces, etc. (Burress, 1980, p. 48)

The self-proclaimed goal of the rehabilitation program was "independence and self-care," and the programs were designed for Ghanaians with disabilities in both urban areas and "small villages throughout the countryside." Vocational rehabilitation programs were run by the Ministries of Labor, Social Welfare, Community Development, and Cooperatives. There were also advisory committees at the regional and national levels with representation from the Ghana Employers Association and the Trade Union Congress. The

German Government "is providing substantial management and operational support for two industrial training and production centers." The Biriwa center "had been substantially enlarged to provide a furniture and manufacturing and dressmaking operation," and school officials had developed a poultry farm and a community farm. These initiatives led at least one international disability organization to recommend Ghana as a model for other African countries' disability initiatives (Burress, 1980, pp. 49–51).

At this time, Ghana's rehabilitation program included the nine rehabilitation centers mentioned above as well as an additional urban rehabilitation center in Biriwa, Cape Coast. The Industrial Rehabilitation Center in Accra offered a residential program with training in rug- or bag-making, copy-typing, rural crafts, carpentry, metal work, joinery or furniture making, shoe-making or shoe repair, and tailoring. The Vocational Training Rehabilitation Center in Biriwa emphasized rural employment and self-employment, "offering basic skills training in building construction, metal work, wood carving and art crafts." The Rural Rehabilitation Training Centers offered a variety of programs for rural development, including "home craft skills, dressmaking, kente cloth weaving/dyeing, leatherwork, seagrass weaving, farming, poultry raising, shoemaking and tailoring." Other state-run centers included the Young Men's Christian Association (YMCA). Trade Training Center, the Occupational Industrial Training Center, the Home and School for Children with mental health conditions, and the State School for the Deaf (all in Accra), as well as the Akropong School for the Blind, the Mampong School for the Deaf, and the Mampong Teacher Training Centre. These state institutions were complemented by a network of private DPOs, including the Ghana Society for the Blind, the Ghana Cripples Aid Society, the Ghana Society for the Deaf, the Society of Friends of Mentally Retarded Children, the Society of Friends of Lepers, the Society for the Prevention of Tuberculosis, and St. Joseph's Hospital, which had a prosthetic limb and brace shop (Buress, 1980, pp. 49–50).

In addition to making Ghana a leader in disability programs in Africa, these initiatives also signaled a turn toward human rights. Indeed, the editors of a 1981 collection of papers from a disability conference in Cape Coast tied the publication directly to the rights approach of the UN by alluding to the International Year of Disabled Persons. The conference was sponsored by the World Rehabilitation Fund (USA), the Ghana Education Service, the Ghana Department of Social Welfare, and the University of Cape Coast, and, while it reflected the medical model's focus on rehabilitation, it also included contributions on social model issues such as independent living, and it is infused with the language of human rights. The conference and publication anticipated the continuation of Ghana's disability programs, and the Ghanaian presenters looked forward to strengthening the government's work on disability prevention, assessment of disabilities, rehabilitation, and economic integration (Marfo et al., 1983). It seemed like a very good time for disability policy in Ghana.

But then came J. J. Rawlings' coup of December 1981, followed by a serious economic crisis and the adoption of structural adjustment in Ghana in the wake of the Berg Report. One important result was that Rawlings' government accepted deep cuts to social spending as a condition of structural adjustment loans. The cuts affected health care, education, and social welfare generally (Brydon & Legge, 1996) and, as such, hurt the disability sector as well. As Geurts observes, Ghana's economic crisis at this time caused "food shortages, extensive unemployment, deterioration of transportation infrastructure and communication networks, environmental degradation, and declining health and social welfare systems" (Geurts, 2015).

Also, the economic collapse impacted disability programs. For instance, the Accra Rehabilitation Centre "became progressively dilapidated; no government agency took responsibility for its upkeep. What little attention it received came from the original renters—Ghana Society for the Blind—and this was through charitable giving on the part of a proliferating array of internationally sponsored NGOs." The center—and presumably other disability centers—became one of a network of government distribution sites for essential goods. According to the head of the GAB at the time, Eleazar Plahar,

> In 1983–84, that's when we had our rule of the Provisional National Defence Council (PNDC). So, life was very difficult and most of the members who were coming [to meetings, to The Centre], they were coming because of items that you could secure. Our government was distributing items through organized societies. (Geurts, 2015)

Internationally, the UN's International Decade of Disabled Persons went ahead as planned from 1983 to 1992, and it nurtured the continued development of the disability movement in Ghana, controlled at the grassroots by persons with disabilities themselves. A good example related to people with physical disabilities, who created their own organization, the Ghana Society of the Physically Disabled (GSPD), in the 1980s. Geurts presents the story of the founding of GPSD:

> In relating an origin story to me, one of the founders, Attakora Asamoa, explained, "The blind had their own organization, and the deaf had their own organization, but nothing existed for physically disabled people." In the context of food rationing, this kind of self-help/support group was crucial for survival. He also cited a Ghanaian proverb to emphasize the significance of this development for people with physical disabilities: "He who wears the shoe knows where it pinches." (Geurts, 2015)

The UN Decade on Disability also called for member countries to create umbrella organizations for their DPOs, which could serve as vehicles for developing national disability legislation. Ghanaian DPOs worked with the Norwegian Agency for Development Cooperation (NORAD) to create of the Federation of Disabled Associations (FODA) in 1988, which eventually became the Ghana Federation of the Disabled (GFD)—now Ghana Federation of Disability Organisations. NORAD also provided funding to establish a new rehabilitation center in Kumasi. Meanwhile, Rawlings' government took some steps to support disability programs, including the formation in 1985 of the Special Education Division within the Ghana Education Service (GES) (Anthony, 2009).

Moving ahead to the 1990s, the Ghanaian government adopted a new Constitution in 1992, after a controversial democratic election, which contained some provisions for disability rights. Three articles in particular related to disability: Article 29, which provided for protection from discrimination and abusive treatment and stated that Ghanaians with disabilities were to be "made to feel an integral part of society"; Article 37, which mandated the legislature to enact appropriate laws relating to disability; and Article 38, which mandated free and compulsory basic education for all children, including, by implication, children with disabilities (Anthony, 2009). The main strategy for achieving these goals in the 1990s was Community Based Rehabilitation (CBR), an approach created by the WHO in 1978 to extend rehabilitation services in "resource-constrained settings" by utilizing local resources and encouraging the participation of community members, including individuals with disabilities themselves (World Health Organization, n.d.). The Ghanaian government started a national CBR program in 1992, administered by the Ministry of Employment and Social Welfare with the participation of the Ministries of Health and Education, and support from the Swedish Organizations of Disabled Persons International Aid Association (SHIA), the Norwegian Association of the Disabled (NAD), as well as the WHO, ILO, and UNESCO. The program fit with Rawlings' move to decentralize government services and development. Its main activities included the employment and training of district Community Based Rehabilitation (CBR) Agents and local voluntary supervisors, the establishment of Community CBR Committees, the employment and training of district teachers who support inclusive education in schools, and the training of staff in health, education, and social welfare departments. Lawrence Ofori Addo from the Accra Rehabilitation Center (ARC) coordinated the CBR program, and this important role helped the ARC to become a hub of capacity building for DPOs, and disability advocacy focused on lobbying the government to pass a national disability act (Geurts, 2015).

Special education initiatives also continued to develop in Ghana during the 1990s. Segregated schools dominated the sector. As of 1992, the country had seventeen specialized schools: twelve for the deaf, two for the blind, and three for children with developmental disabilities. All of these schools except two for the blind were residential, although the two non-residential day schools, which served deaf students, supported their students by subsidizing meals and transportation (Mantey, 2017). At the same time, the Government of Ghana signaled a commitment to Inclusive Education (IE) by accepting the World Bank's Education for All initiative of 1990 and signing UNESCO's 1994 Salamanca Statement on Inclusive Education (Deku & Vanderpuye, 2017). As defined by the WHO and World Bank, "inclusive education entails identifying and removing barriers, and providing reasonable accommodation to enable every child to participate and achieve within mainstream educational settings" (World Health Organization and World Bank, 2011, p. 108). While Ghana's big push for IE did not happen until the early 2000s, the government's acceptance of the World Bank and UNESCO programs set the process in motion during the 1990s (Deku & Venderpuye, 2017).

At the international level, events at the UN during the 1990s set the scene for disability activists to lobby the UN for a new convention on disability rights. A major step occurred in 1993 with the publication of Leandro Despouy's *Report on Disability and Human Rights*. The report contained elements of the social model, such as Despouy's statement that "the treatment given to disabled [*sic*] persons defines the innermost characteristics of a society and highlights the cultural values that sustain it" (Despouy, 1993, par. 5). The social model also infused Despouy's strong stance against cultural and social discrimination. However, in locating discrimination entirely in the realm of culture and society, Despouy detached social model language from its materialist base and absorbed it into an idealist formulation. As a result, the report's recommendations reiterated the medical model's focus on rehabilitation into "normal" life but added the idea that this would require changes in social and cultural beliefs and attitudes (Despouy, 1993). The UN carried this hybrid medical and social approach forward into the Standard Rules on the Equalization of Opportunities for Disabled Persons, adopted by the General Assembly on December 20, 1993.

Following Despouy's report, the next major step toward the United Nations implemented its Convention on the Rights of Persons with Disabilities (CRPD) occurred in 2001, when the Mexican members of the UN General Assembly sponsored a General Assembly resolution calling for the establishment of an Ad Hoc Committee (AHC),

> to consider proposals for a comprehensive and integral international convention to promote and protect the rights and dignity of persons with disabilities, based on the holistic approach in the work done in the fields of social development, human rights and non-discrimination and taking into account the

> recommendations of the Commission on Human Rights and the Commission for Social Development. (Guernsey et al., 2017)

Most of the resolution's co-sponsors were from the Global South, reflecting the rise of the transnational disability movement sparked by the formation of DPI in 1981 (Guernsey et al., 2017). From Africa, the Working Group of the AHC, which was tasked with drafting the CRPD, had representatives from seven countries: Cameroon, Comoros, Mali, Morocco, Sierra Leone, South Africa, and Uganda (Lord & Stein, 2013). The AHC met eight times between 2002 and 2006 at the UN Headquarters in New York, at times breaking off into sub-units. After producing a number of preliminary and draft texts, the AHC finalized the CRPD in August 2006 and forwarded it to the General Assembly, where it was adopted on December 13, 2006 (Guernsey et al., 2017). As Gooding observes, the CRPD therefore "represents the culmination of two and a half decades of development in international human rights law aimed at addressing human rights violations experienced by people with disabilities" (Gooding, 2014). It was also the most quickly negotiated human rights treaty in the history of the United Nations (United Nations, 2015).

In Ghana, the international surge toward disability rights set the scene for sustained activity by DPOs, including those located at the Accra Rehabilitation Center, which pressured the government to adopt disability rights legislation. Geurts captures the spirit of the times very vividly. "During the first decade of the 21st century," she writes, "The Centre was a hub of activist energy aimed at political and social changes that would create better worlds for people with disabilities. Like a vortex, it spawned and preserved emergent forces" (Geurts, 2015). The center launched income-generation projects, and the GFD welcomed new DPOs into its fold, including the Parents Association of Children with Intellectual Disabilities in 2001, the Society of Albinos Ghana in 2003, and Sharecare Ghana (focusing on "rare neuro-immunological diseases") in 2006 (Geurts, 2015). Advocacy efforts by DPOs also helped to convince the government to implement a National Disability Policy in June 2000, which set out rights for Ghanaians with disabilities in line with the UN's Standard Rules of 1993, including "education, transportation, community acceptance, housing and employment" (Anthony, 2009). The government also developed an Education Strategic Plan between 2003 and 2015, which included the creation of thirty-five inclusive schools. Perhaps most importantly, after two years of lobbying supported by a grant from the Rights and Voice Initiative (RAVI), GFD succeeded in pressing the Ghanaian government to develop a formal Disability Act, which it passed in 2006 (Geurts, 2015).

While Ghana was moving toward increased disability rights, the CRPD opened for signatures in 2006. The Convention is an interesting document that affected disability issues in diverse ways in Ghana. On the one hand, it contains language consistent with the social model, including the statements that "everyone is entitled to all the rights and freedoms set forth (in the UN Declaration of Human Rights) without distinction of any kind" (United Nations, 2006, Preamble [b]) and that

> disability is an evolving concept and . . . results from the interaction between persons with impairments and attitudinal and environmental barriers that hinders their full and effective participation in society on an equal basis with others. (United Nations, 2006, Preamble [e])

From here, the CRPD goes on to mandate rights in areas such as justice, healthcare, and employment. For example, on justice, the CRPD establishes the right to "effective access to justice for persons with disabilities" (United Nations, 2006, Art. 1, 11). On health care, the CRPD stipulates equal rights to "free or affordable" access to medical treatment, including disability-specific services (United Nations, 2006, Art 25(a), (b), (c)). It also mandates State Parties to promote rehabilitation programs, including the provision and training in the use of "assistive devices" at an "affordable cost" (United Nations, 2006, Art 26(3), 20(a), 20(b)). On employment, the CRPD includes non-discrimination and equal pay for equal work, as well as the rights to "reasonable accommodation" and return-to-work programs for individuals "who acquire a disability during the course of employment" (United Nations, 2006, Art 27(1) (a, i, k)). Other notable articles speak to self-determination and independent decision-making (Article 12), liberty, security, and protection from arbitrary detention (Article 14), and a sanction against involuntary medical treatment (Article 17). The CRPD also calls on State Parties to undertake awareness-raising campaigns to combat stereotypes, discrimination, and abuse of persons with disabilities worldwide (United Nations, 2006, Art 12, 14, 17, 8(1a), 9(2d)).

The CRPD generally privileges attitude change as the foundation for helping State Parties to enforce civil rights for persons with disabilities, to allow them to integrate into so-called "normal" society. This approach has been criticized by radical disability activists such as Marta Russell, who argues that, as a liberal civil rights instrument, the CRPD forces disability issues into an individual rights framework within existing power structures under neoliberal regimes (Russell, 2002). This runs the risk of limiting the benefits at the grassroots to already-powerful individuals with disabilities, or at least to individuals who have connections to more powerful patrons. In an example from Ghana, Grischow provides evidence for this reality in a case study of an individual who acquired disabilities after a motorcycle accident and needed to access patron-client networks to obtain essential benefits (Grischow, 2015). But even for those who can tap into the CRPD's provisions in their home countries in Africa, they almost certainly will face even financial barriers to disability imposed by the rights-providers (governments, employers, et cetera) under neoliberal policies, than Americans with disabilities encounter with the ADA, for example. Research on Ghana has shown this to be true for basic rights, including employment (especially for Ghanaian women with disabilities) and drinking water (Dosu & Hanrahan, 2021). In other words, the CRPD and its associated African disability rights instruments might be a very positive step forward for some persons with disabilities in Africa, but most likely only for a small minority, who have the resources to secure disability rights under neoliberalism.

Beyond these issues, while the CRPD represents a positive step away from the medical model, it also rejects the political economy approach of the original Finklestein/Oliver conception of the social model. In the radical critique based on this model, the CRPD's focus on removing barriers by changing attitudes "diverts attention from the mode of production and the concrete social relations that produce the disabling barriers, exclusion and inequalities facing disabled persons" (Russell & Malhotra, 2002, p. 212). In this light, "disability" is produced socially to the extent that persons with impairments are barred from the labor market. Moreover, as surplus laborers, they are functional to capitalism (Russell & Malhotra, 2002). According to this school of thought, a liberal human rights instrument like the CRPD might allow a minority of persons with disabilities to enter the workforce, but it will do little if anything to change the system that keeps most persons with disabilities at the very bottom of the surplus labor pool. They will have rights on paper, but not in practice. Even for those who can enter the labor market, they will only have earned the right to be exploited by capital. In other words, rights-based approaches run the risk of seeking "to challenge and eliminate discrimination not exploitation" (Di Stafano, 2015).

CONCLUSION

The history of disability in Ghana provides a backdrop against which to assess contemporary experiences of stigma and discrimination. This chapter has reconstructed elements of that history from the precolonial period through to independence. Due to the lack of scholarship on the earliest eras, it was important to include the entire African continent in the discussion. Even then, very few sources exist that can produce a definitive analysis of precolonial disability stigma. Still, it is possible to draw several conclusions from the evidence that exists. First, we can say with some certainty that stigma existed toward persons with disabilities in precolonial Africa and also in Ghana, as evidenced by proverbs that have been collected and published. The oral traditions that have been passed down include stories that portray persons with disabilities as inferior and not worthy of social inclusion. However, we also find evidence of social inclusion, especially in the case of Muslim African societies which had rules and norms providing persons with disabilities with certain rights and privileges. This phenomenon was perhaps strongest for blindness, and it included West African societies in savannah areas not far from present-day Ghana.

The historical record becomes stronger for the colonial period, at least with respect to rehabilitation and education programs as necessary steps toward the economic inclusion—and by extension, social inclusion—of persons with disabilities in Africa and Ghana specifically. World War II was a watershed moment in this process. Responding to the impact of disabling wartime injuries among European and colonial soldiers, the British government designed and implemented rehabilitation programs in the United Kingdom and the African colonies. These programs included a rehabilitation center in Ghana, which began in the late 1940s. The same era witnessed the rise of special schools for Ghanaians with disabilities, including deaf and blind schools. The ultimate goal of these schools was also to train persons with disabilities for participation in the workforce. The legacy of rehabilitation and education continued after independence in 1957. Under the first prime minister of independent Ghana, Kwame Nkrumah, the special schools expanded, and major surveys of disability were undertaken across the country. The latter led to the establishment and expansion of rehabilitation centers, mainly for blind persons, under the management of the British Empire Society for the Blind. During the late 1960s, graduates of the blind and deaf schools struck out on their own to form grassroots organizations controlled and operated by persons with disabilities themselves and dedicated to achieving disability rights. They were joined by persons with physical disabilities, who created their own organization in the 1980s. The movement toward disability rights accelerated after the CRPD in 2006. The same year witnessed the implementation of a national disability Act in Ghana, and in 2012, the Ghanaian government also ratified the CRPD. The ratification of the CRPD ushered in the era of disability rights in Ghana.

Tracing this history is important as a backdrop to the analysis that follows. First, it shows that traditional attitudes toward disability in Ghana include both stigma and acceptance. Second, the history of disability in Ghana reveals a deeply ingrained colonial approach to disability that focuses on the need for rehabilitation and reintegration of persons with disabilities into the workforce. Third, the more recent experience with disability highlights the shift from charity to a human rights approach to disability in Ghana that has arisen since 2006. All of these themes should be kept in mind as the analysis shifts to the contemporary experience of stigma in chapters 2–5.

NOTES

1. Perceived causes of disability and attitudes toward persons with disabilities will be discussed separately below.

2. Both resolutions were products of their time, adopting the paternalistic language of the medical model as well as its focus on individual rehabilitation and "normalizing" disabled bodies. For instance, the 1971 resolution set out the right to "integration *as far as possible in normal life*" (emphasis added) and declared that persons with developmental disabilities had "the same rights as other human beings," but only "to the maximum degree of feasibility." The 1975 Resolution defined disability in terms of "deficiency, either congenital or not, in . . . physical or mental capabilities" and focused on rights such as "medical and social rehabilitation" and vocational training. Both declarations stated that an individual with disabilities could have their rights revoked if a panel of experts decided that the disability was too severe. United Nations (1971, 1975).

Part II

EXPERIENCING DISABILITY AND DISABILITY STIGMA

Chapter 2

Culture and Disability in Ghana

INTRODUCTION

Oftentimes, culture—the way of life of a people (Anbaran, 2016; Eskay et al., 2012)—influences what people believe about and how they relate with a phenomenon. Culture names and gives meaning to a phenomenon and guides how society navigates the phenomenon to derive benefits from it and/or avoid its negative side. Culture defines what is desirable and undesirable, and in most Ghanaian cases, phenomena like disability have been defined and characterized negatively with concomitant negative effects on persons who experience them (Moasun, 2023; Moasun & Mfoafo-M'Carthy, 2021). Devlieger (2015) profoundly makes the case that in Africa, the name given to a particular kind of disability initiates a socialization process that determines and shapes the ways persons with disabilities experience their bodies and, to a significant extent, how they experience personhood. Some aspects of African cultures may impact positively on how persons with disabilities experience their conditions (Eskay et al., 2012).

However, our many years of research and observations suggest that Ghanaian cultures and their dictates on disability predominantly portray disability negatively, resulting often in negative experiences for persons with disabilities and, to a large extent, members of their families or caregivers—the subject of discussion in chapter 5 of this book. Ghanaian cultures have contributed to the naming and shaping of relationships with persons with disabilities that can best be described as restrictive, derogatory, and retrogressive. Culture is often central to the negative experiences of personhood for persons with disabilities, as many of them tend to experience negative social, economic, cultural, and religious citizenships. The inability of persons with disabilities to participate in life-defining activities of society partially or fully, such as the above, means their overall quality of life is significantly lower compared to that of the general population (Kuvalekar et al., 2015; Rajati et al., 2018). In this chapter, we draw on literature from the broader African context and interviews from fieldwork in Ghana to discuss different aspects of culture and their effects on how persons with disabilities, including those with mental illness, experience their conditions within the Ghanaian society.

CULTURE AND ITS CHARACTERISTICS

In order to effectively situate this chapter, it is imperative to quickly define and characterize culture. While culture is iterative and yet varied in different geopolitical spaces, there is a common understanding of the concept and its role in determining the lives and experiences of different groups of people within such geopolitical spaces. Broadly, culture is defined as a complex interaction of traditional behaviors that have been developed and learned by different generations of a group of people over time (Mead, 2002). According to Meyer (2017), culture represents those shared systems of values, beliefs, attitudes, norms, and practices common to a group of people. Kroeber and Kluckhohn (1952) define culture as consisting of "patterned ways of thinking, feeling and reacting, acquired and transmitted mainly by symbols, constituting the distinctive achievements of human groups, including their embodiments in artifacts" (p. 86).

Birukou et al. (2013) conceptualize culture as the integration of traditions, knowledge, beliefs, norms, values, behaviors, attitudes, principles, meanings, faith, spatial relations, language, and possessions collectively owned by a society, which are passed on from one generation to another. Culture gives a people their identity and sense of self (Meyer, 2017). Yet, it is not something one is born with, but something one learns over time as one is introduced to, and lives within, a society over time (Birukou et al., 2013; Guffey et al., 2013; Meyer, 2017).

Culture has several characteristics which impact the lives of the people who live it. Some of these characteristics have been outlined by Guffey et al. (2013), including:

- Culture is shaped by attitudes that are learned in childhood and internalized as individuals age into adulthood.
- The rules, values, and attitudes of a culture are learned and transferred from one generation to another.
- Cultural practices are inherently logical for the people who hold and enact their cultural values, norms, and attitudes.

- Culture is the basis for how a community identifies itself to the world. It determines a community's sense of identity and togetherness.
- Culture is not static. It is dynamic and changes over time. Some cultural changes may be rapid, while other changes happen incrementally over a long period of time.
- Some aspects of culture may be tangible or visible such as artifacts, while other aspects may be invisible, such as values, norms, and languages.

Culture may impact various groups of people in society differently. Usually, dominant groups with power tend to benefit positively from culture, while vulnerable populations, such as those with disabilities, tend to face different disadvantages of dominant culture (Bourdieu, 1990). While culture may evolve over time, its effects are deep-rooted and nearly indelible. Hence, the impressions that culture creates on a people can become deeply entrenched, with dire consequences for different segments of society. In most societies across the world, when culture combines with religious and spiritual belief systems—which is often the case—its impact on different aspects of society becomes complicated and difficult, if not impossible, to undo.

In Africa, there is a strong belief in disability as punishment from supernatural forces such as God the Supreme Being, the spirits of the ancestors, lesser gods, or witchcraft (Agbenyega, 2003; Haihambo & Lightfoot, 2010; Setume, 2016). Where this is the case, it becomes almost impossible for members of society to want to associate positively with persons with disabilities for fear of incurring the displeasures of the already angry spirits. Thus, in Ghana and most parts of the Global South, culture and its elements of religion and spirituality have acted to define and dictate relationships with persons with disabilities in often negative ways. Subsequently, this chapter focuses on aspects of culture, such as language, and their consequential impact on the lives of persons with disabilities in Ghana.

LANGUAGE AS A CULTURAL TOOL AND ITS IMPACT ON DISABILITY

Language is a key cultural heritage across the world. The United Nations Educational, Scientific, and Cultural Organization [UNESCO] (2003) characterizes it as an intangible cultural heritage. In its Convention for Safeguarding Intangible Cultural Heritage, UNESCO defines intangible cultural heritage as "the practices, representations, expressions, knowledge, skills—as well as the instruments, objects, artefacts and cultural spaces associated therewith—that communities, groups and, in some cases, individuals recognize as part of their cultural heritage" (p. 4). Mediums such as performing arts; social practices, rituals, and festive events; knowledge and practices concerning nature and the universe; and traditional craftsmanship (UNESCO, 2003) are among the most perceptible cultural manifestations.

Language in its various forms, including oral traditions and expressions, is an important manifestation of intangible cultural heritages (UNESCO, 2003). Kurin (2004), in his appraisal of the UNESCO Convention for Safeguarding Intangible Cultural Heritage, elaborates the linguistic elements of culture to include epics, folktales, stories, and folklore. Another way that culture is expressed through music is ancient or folk music. Smeets (2004) contends that language is a rule that plays an indispensable role in the identities of groups and individuals. The power of language as a cultural tool is evidenced in the role it plays in naming and bringing phenomena to life.

To the foregoing effect, language plays an indispensable role in defining and centering a people's cultural identity. Identity, on the other hand, plays a significant role in the way that others within and outside the culture relate with individuals impacted by the identity. Therefore, names given to concepts or phenomena within a culture are important. The name given to a phenomenon sets up the rules of engagement with the phenomenon; it directs and guides relationships and behaviors about the phenomenon. A name that is given to a phenomenon may dictate the desirability or otherwise of the phenomenon. It is because of the power of language to define and dictate relationships around concepts that disability scholars have been concerned about the intentional use of disability language in order to prevent negative representations that have consequences for persons with disabilities (Devlin & Pothier, 2006).

In Africa, disability language is still being developed. In many African languages, there are often references to impairments in body parts rather than specific names for disability as a phenomenon (Moasun, 2023; Talle, 1995). This way of presenting disability may be the reason for the predominantly derogatory names that are given to impairments and, by extension, disability in most African languages. It is worth noting that when impairments are given derogatory names, there is a high likelihood that people who bear these impairments will encounter negative experiences in their interactions with members of their societies. Devlieger (2015) points out that in providing the name to a disability, culture "provides the individual with disability with the beginning of a socialization process that will shape their bodily experience of difference" (p. 79). He iterates that it is within the naming process of any phenomenon that culture plays a role by providing meaning to the phenomenon. Hence, the label that is given to an impairment becomes the way by which the individual is identified in society and determines how members of society relate with the individual. This means the label guides society's choices as to whether to accept or reject the individual (Agbenyega, 2003).

Ghanaian Disability Terminologies

The power of disability labeling gives rise to concern in the Ghanaian context. A cursory scan of disability terminology among Ghanaian languages from literature affirms this concern. Many local disability terminologies are derogatory, and where this is not the case, they present the concept as a sickness. In Likpakpaaln,[1] a person with a disability is predominantly referred to as “ubun,” and among the Akans and the Gas, they are respectively referred to as “yarefo and helats ɛ,” to wit, sick persons (Moasun, 2023; Nepveux, 2009). Again, in Likpakpaaln, a person with impairments in the legs is called “uwab,” which means the “wrecked one.” Naami (2012) affirms that among the Nchumburu of the Northern and Oti regions of Ghana, such a person is referred to as “kejabo,” meaning “crippled,” and a person with hearing difficulties is called “kpawu,” which means “dumb” (Naami, 2012, p. 101). Agbenyega (2003, p. 4) indicates that among the Ewe ethnic group of Ghana and Togo, a person with epilepsy is called “dzeanyikplatowo.” This term, as Agbenyega explains, is derogatory and translates as “falling down sicknesses.” Agbenyega further indicates that cataract among the Ewe people is known as “kobi,” which comes with the belief that the individual with the eye condition is facing punishments from the gods for offenses committed by them or their families.

Again, Agbenyega (2003) explains that among the Ewe and Ga ethnic groups, persons with mental or intellectual disabilities are referred to as “Asotowo” and “Buluu,” respectively. Both terms translate literally as “idiots” or “fools.” In a similar vein, among the Akans, they refer to a person with an intellectual disability as “nea wanyin agya n’adwene no”—translated as the one who has outgrown his or her mind or thought processes. In other words, the “feeble minded” (Agbenyega, 2003). Baffoe (2013, p. 193) indicates that “[P]ersons with Autism and Down’s Syndrome” are labeled as “kwasea, kwasea” “gyimi gyimi.” Meaning, “stupid person or imbecile.” Across the West African region, children with varying disabilities are referred to as spirit, bad, evil, snake, or river children (Allotey and Reidpath, 2001; Bayat, 2015; Botts and Evans, 2010; Denham et al., 2010; Kassah et al., 2012; Oppong-Ansah, 2011). These referents render persons with disabilities unrelatable. It is a no-brainer that anyone will want to have anything to do with a person who is believed to be evil, or a child of a river or snake. As we will see later in this chapter, disability language, as discussed in this and the foregoing paragraph, together with other cultural factors set persons with disabilities up for marginalization and dis-citizenship[2].

Ghanaian Proverbs and Disability

Apart from direct linguistic labeling that produces negative consequences for persons with disabilities, proverbs are a critical element of language with the potential to negatively affect persons with disabilities (Moasun & Mfoafo-M'Carthy, 2021). This is because proverbs play a significant role in sustaining and propagating culture (Archer, 1931; Magwaza, 2004; Mensah, 2017). Magwaza (2004) posits proverbs to be derived from "beliefs, values, attitudes, perceptions, emotions and the entire system of thoughts and feelings" (p. 37) of the people. The import of proverbs in understanding disability is particularly significant because proverbs are static and their narratives are nearly impossible to change (Alemu, 2007). In chapter 2, we used proverbs to demonstrate the historical understanding of disability and relationships with persons with disabilities in Ghana. Here, we seek to repeat some of the proverbs as used in the preceding chapter to demonstrate how, as an element of culture, proverbs contribute to stigma and discrimination against persons with disabilities. When proverbs are effectively employed, they embellish speech and make it pleasant for the listener. As this happens, proverbs leave indelible impressions in the minds of the listener. Chinua Achebe, a renowned Nigerian writer, in his world-acclaimed book *Things Fall Apart* speaks of the role of proverbs in everyday speech as being "the palm-oil with which words are eaten" (Achebe, 1997, p. 4). To this effect, proverbs can be employed as ways to minimize the direct impact of negative expressions on recipients of the messages. However, they could be employed in a negative sense that has the potential to hurt the listener and the object of the conversation.

Moasun and Mfoafo-M'Carthy (2021) make the case, and we have already demonstrated in chapter 2 that proverbs are fictional imaginations but emanate from historical antecedents within a people's culture. Thus, we emphasize here that proverbs represent cultural realities and, in relation to disability, they represent realities of the experiences of persons with disabilities. For example, the proverb that "*A bad* [evil] *child, we kill through the fetish priest*" conveys a message that, within the Akan culture, there are certain children who are perceived to be bad, and the fate of such children is often murder. This perception of some children is not exclusive to Akan communities. It is pervasive across Ghana.

Literature shows that in many Ghanaian societies, the "bad child" is one who is born with a difference (Allotey & Reidpath, 2001; Botts & Evans, 2010; Denham et al., 2010; Moasun, 2019). Such children include those born with microcephaly, macrocephaly, hydrocephalus, missing limbs, teeth in their mouth, a tiny sixth finger, facial hair, or other secondary sex characteristics, among others (Denham et al., 2010). Research and anecdotal evidence suggest that across Ghana, many of these children are either directly killed or neglected to die (Allotey & Reidpath, 2001; Botts & Evans, 2010; Denham et al., 2010; Moasun, 2019). Hence, despite the interpretation of the proverb by Appiah et al. (2007) to mean "we use clever means to get rid of a difficult person" (p. 20), the evidence in literature indicates to the contrary that the proverb has a literal meaning, which is that within Ghanaian societies, there are certain children who are considered evil or bad and some of these children are in fact killed.

Another example of proverbs and their negative cultural impressions of persons with disabilities is the one spoken of persons with angular kyphosis to the effect that "If you chase a hunchback and you don't succeed, it is not because of his swiftness but because of his laughable figure" (Appiah et al., 2007, p. 242). Stigma and discrimination against persons with angular kyphosis are pervasive in present-day Ghana, just as they might have been at the time this proverb first emerged and was employed in speech within Ghanaian societies. First, the proverb portrays that persons with angular kyphosis are subjects of mockery in their communities. Second, there is an explicit communication that such individuals lack the ability to outrun other persons who chase after them. The following excerpt from one of our studies on disability in Ghana sees a woman with angular kyphosis desisting from participating in cultural dance because she is constantly subjected to mockery when she attempts to dance:

> *Even if I am walking, they laugh at me, how then should I court trouble for myself by trying to dance? They will laugh at me, so I don't go there at all. I don't even get motivated to dance. . . . Deep down my heart, I see how they are dancing, and I want to dance but I cannot. . . . I can see my condition, I cannot dance [laughs aloud].*

In the first place, the above excerpt confirms the messages in proverbs are not fictional but based on the realities of people's experiences. It also confirms that persons with angular kyphosis in Ghanaian communities are often mocked. Notice that the woman premises her decision not to attempt dancing on the fact that, by going about her normal life, she gets laughed at when she walks. This speaks to how endemic this negative attitude is. While such stigmatizing attitudes may prevent persons with disabilities from active participation in community life, we see from the excerpt above that the woman involved has internalized the label and succumbed to the pressure exerted on her by such negative attitudes. Like Rokach et al. (2006) have suggested, most persons with disabilities tend to self-alienate when they are unable to sustain societal stigma and discrimination.

For our third example to demonstrate how proverbs convey culture and its influence on disability, let us analyze the proverb "one never commiserates with a cripple's mother." As indicated in chapter 1, Appiah et al. (2007) interpret this proverb to mean, "It should be taken for granted that you are sorry for someone unfortunate. By calling attention to it, you make it worse" (Appiah et al., 2007, p. 38). This proverb is an affirmation of the Ghanaian perception of disability as a tragedy that is worth mourning. According to the proverb, children born with physical impairments are viewed as misfortunes to their mothers. This reaction to the existence of a child with physical impairments typifies the tragedy model of disability (Retief & Letšosa, 2018) and calls for pity for the mother of the child. We see from the proverb that emphasis is on commiserating with the mother and not on the well-being of the child. This is suggestive of the fact that value may not be placed on the lives of such children, and so their survival may be a major concern. When a child is perceived as a tragedy to his or her mother, there is an implication that the mere existence of the child may invoke resentments from their mothers and/or other members of their families. This could be one of the reasons children born with bodily differences, as discussed earlier, are killed (Allotey & Reidpath, 2001; Botts & Evans, 2010; Denham et al., 2010; Moasun, 2019).

As we draw the curtains on this section, it is important to acknowledge that there are a few Ghanaian proverbs that promote inclusion for persons with disabilities. The proverb "It is because of Obiri that we drink the drink [wine] of the one-armed man" (Appiah et al., 2007, p. 48) means that while culture appears to be static, it is still amenable to change. This proverb confirms that a lot of the stigma that persons with disabilities face in Ghanaian societies is socially constructed and can be deconstructed with political will and commitment. It is a reminder that where leadership gives a positive outlook to disability and positively relates with individuals with disabilities, they will inspire the sociocultural and attitudinal changes necessary for the de-stigmatization and inclusion of persons with disabilities in society. This will eventually lead to their empowerment.

The foregoing discussion positions language as an essential element of culture with a symbiotic relationship with dominant belief systems. Language can inform belief systems and is itself informed by belief systems. When language and belief systems combine, they can have telling effects on vulnerable populations, such as those with disabilities. In the next section, we discuss some African and Ghanaian beliefs about disabilities and persons with disabilities and how these can impact individuals with disabilities in society.

INDIGENOUS BELIEFS ABOUT IMPAIRMENTS AND DISABILITIES

Religion, spirituality, and belief systems are essential components of a people's culture (Edara, 2017). In most African and, for that matter, Ghanaian cultures, there is an intricate connection between the physical and the spiritual, such that life cannot be lived meaningfully without a good balance between the two realms. This connection is demonstrated by beliefs in the spirits of the ancestors and the significant roles they play in the day-to-day lives of the people. For example, Moasun (2019) describes the indispensable roles played by various spirits—God, ancestors, and smaller gods—in maintaining social order among the Bikpakpaam (Konkomba people) of Northern Ghana. In this exposition, he indicates that the power that Bikpakpaam Elders use to govern their people is derived from the spirits of their ancestors. Thus, the Elder is essentially a messenger and the mouthpiece of the ancestors.

In essence, instructions issued by the Elder are followed not only out of respect for him but also largely out of the fear of the wrath of the ancestors who are the issuants of the instructions. This example demonstrates the role spirituality plays in the creation, shaping, and maintenance of culture. Moasun (2019) emphasizes the powerful impact of spirituality even on the existence of humanity among Bikpakpaam when he indicated that the birth of every infant occasioned the consultation of soothsayers and fetish priests to determine its faith as qualified or not qualified to live. This consultation has dire implications for infants who are born with features that deviate from what is normal to the people. It is in this regard that Devlieger (2015) stresses that, "[L]ocal African concepts of disability reflect the boundaries of a worldview that includes ideas of life and death, this world and the supernatural, social relations, causal attributions, and a categorization of the extraordinary body" (p. 91). Thus, disability is understood as both a physical and spiritual phenomena.

Extant literature suggests that in most communities in Africa, including Ghana, the birth of a healthy (desirable) child is a sign of harmony between this world and the supernatural one (Mbiti, 1991). On the other hand, the birth of a child who appears differently gives rise to various, often unfavorable interpretations, such as fears of infractions between the people and the spirits (Allotey & Reidpath, 2001; Bayat, 2015; Denham et al., 2010; Fiasorgbor & Ayagiyire, 2015; Kiyaga & Moores, 2003; Slikker, 2009). In many societies in Ghana, it is believed that the misdeeds of the parents can incur the anger of the spirits, who punish them with children who have deformities (Allotey & Reidpath, 2001; Botts & Evans, 2010; Denham et al., 2010). Agbenyega (2003) explains that among Ghanaians, it is believed that parents can spiritually exchange a part of the body of their child for money, which can result in physical defects. Agbenyega (2003) also indicates that some societies in Ghana believe that animals such as snakes and crocodiles have special powers to punish people who are mean to them by causing them to give birth to children who have deformities.

While large-scale research on the topic is nonexistent, a small-scale research project by Fiasorgbor and Ayagiyire (2015) on fifty participants revealed that 68 percent of the sample believed that a curse on a family could result in the disability of members, while 62 percent believed that evil spirits caused disabilities. Half (50 percent) of the participants believed that divine punishment from God caused disabilities. Despite beliefs in spiritual causes, the study also found that all participants believed that traumatic events could result in disabilities. The study also found that 96 percent of the participants believed that diseases could result in disabilities; 94 percent and 56 percent believed that medical errors and hereditary factors, respectively, could cause disabilities in people. Similarly, a much larger study by Slikker (2009) engaged 400 participants in a survey and found that 90.4 percent of Ghanaian respondents believed that accidents caused disabilities, while 89.1 percent believed diseases caused disabilities. Another 72.8 percent believed that medical errors caused disabilities, and 38.2 percent believed in curses as causes of disabilities (Slikker, 2009).

Epilepsy is one of the most dreaded disabling health conditions among African societies. The dread of the condition is mainly influenced by the belief that it is communicable. However, beliefs that persons who have epilepsy are cursed present serious undercurrents that fuel the stigma around it. Research suggests prevailing beliefs about the causes of the condition include curses, evil spirits, witchcraft, the breaking of taboos, and punishment for social wrongdoings, among others (Adjei et al., 2013; Dugbartey & Barimah, 2013). It is worth noting that the beliefs discussed above are not peculiar to traditional societies.

In 1979, Johnson conducted a study on university students in Ghana and found that up to 28 percent believed that witchcraft was responsible for the cause of epilepsy. Another important point to note is the fact that literature on disability beliefs suggests that across Africa, irrespective of the physical or physiological explanations for the occurrence of an impairment that leads to a disability, there remain strong beliefs that all causes of disabilities have spiritual or divine undertones (Devlieger, 1999; Kisanji, 1995; Kiyaga & Moores, 2003). The belief is that if the spirits do not permit it, an event that results in impairment will not occur.

As we ponder over these beliefs about disability, it is important that we begin to reflect on why there is a need to know these. At the core of the subject of protection of the rights of persons with disabilities are the beliefs people have about disabilities (Devlin & Pothier, 2006). Beliefs around disabilities and their causes have a direct effect on how persons with disabilities are treated (Boachie-Sarpong, 2012; Ingstad, 1990; Stone-McDonald & Butera, 2014). In the cultural phase of his classification of persons with disabilities, Devlieger (2015) posits that persons with disabilities tend to be identified in relation to other persons within the context of culture. Devlieger proceeds to raise the crucial question of the extent to which "people with bodily differences in a cultural framework are allowed, by contrast, their full humanity, or classified as 'other,' that is outside of the human realm or as more or less human" (p. 80). This brings to question the personhood[3] of persons with disabilities, resulting in various attitudes and treatments, including the killing of those who are considered "outside of the human realm or less human" (Denham et al., 2010; Moasun, 2019).

There are especially those children who are considered nonhuman, who "represent evil, death, and the supernatural world" (Devlieger, 2015, p. 91). Many of these children have bodily features that deviate from what is recognized as "normal" in society. In many societies in West Africa, including Ghana, these children are variously referred to as bad, evil, snake, or river children (Allotey & Reidpath, 2001; Bayat, 2015; Botts & Evans, 2010; Denham et al., 2010; Kassah et al., 2012; Oppong-Ansah, 2011). Bayat (2015) reports the signs of a snake child—most likely a child with cerebral palsy—as described by a participant as follows: "[T]he child had a problem with movement and could not hold his head up. At one year old he was not walking" (p. 6). Agbenyega (2003) clarifies that many of the children who are referred to as river children in Ghana have Down syndrome.

Similarly, children who are regarded as spirit children include those with hydrocephalus, or who have been born with teeth, facial hair, or other secondary sex characteristics, and those born with broken limbs or other deformities (Denham et al., 2010). Devlieger (2015) opines that in some societies, it is believed that spirit children are an invasion by nature that cannot be conquered. In our estimation, these are the children who are being referred to in the first proverb, as discussed in the previous section of this chapter.

We have established earlier in this session the intricate connection between the spiritual and the physical realms, both of which directly impact belief systems in general and specifically, beliefs about disabilities. It is therefore important to re-emphasize two things: first, that spirituality and beliefs are cultural and integral to the way a people perceive and approach life. Hence, once impairments and/or disabilities are believed to be caused by spiritual factors, there is a strong tendency for solutions to conditions to be approached from a spiritual perspective. When this happens, disabling conditions that are physical and demand physical approaches to deal with might aggravate as people look to spiritual solutions. The experience of a research participant in one of our studies vividly buttresses this point:

> *The way it happened, I knew it was a sickness, but . . . They said somebody cast a spell on me and that is why it happened like that. . . . Native healers used herbs to treat it but for a long time, it did not work, then I was taken to the hospital, and they performed surgery on it and then I am now able to manage it. . . . For me, I think it was an ordinary sickness, otherwise, can a spiritual sickness be cured in the hospital?*

Second, the intricate connection between the spiritual and physical realms has implications for relationship with and treatment of persons with disabilities. Where an impairment and a disability are perceived to have resulted from a curse or punishment by a supernatural power, there is an implicit warning for others, including family members, to desist from relating with and caring for the individual involved in a manner that will incur the displeasure of the offended spirit. This therefore sets the person with disability up for marginalization and neglect. Having come to this understanding of how beliefs influence our understanding of disability and our relationships with persons with disabilities, the next section builds on this understanding to discuss some stereotypes and myths emanating from culture and beliefs, and their implications for society's relationship with persons with disabilities.

DISABILITY STEREOTYPES AND MYTHS

Ghanaians, like many African cultures and belief systems, are replete with stereotypes and myths that may influence the stigmatization, marginalization, and discrimination against persons with disabilities. In this section, we discuss some of these stereotypes and myths and how they contribute directly or indirectly to the negative experiences of persons with disabilities. First, we will discuss common stereotypes as they pertain to disability literature across Africa and then narrow the discussion to examples specific to Ghana as they were obtained from our research in Ghana. We will then delve into myths about disability in a similar manner. Our hope is that by the time you conclude your reading of this section, you will appreciate how some of the taken for granted cultural practices as exhibited in language can be sources of maltreatments for persons with disabilities.

Stereotypes

The *Encyclopedia Britannica* defines stereotype as "an often unfair and untrue belief that many people have about all people or things with a particular characteristic." Similarly, the *Oxford Languages Dictionary* defines the concept as "a widely held but fixed and oversimplified image or idea of a particular type of person or thing." This suggests, in the context of disability, that while these stereotypes may be unfair representations of persons with disabilities, they hold sway over what people believe about disability and how they relate with and treat persons with disabilities. Momene (2015) suggests that disability stereotypes project incomplete information and mistaken perceptions that may result in stigma and marginalization for persons with disabilities. Below are some disability stereotypes gleaned from a cursory review of literature on disability stereotypes in Africa (Boachie-Sarpong, 2012; Livingston, 2005; Momene, 2015):

- Persons with disabilities are pitiable and pathetic.
- Persons with disabilities are sinister or evil.
- Persons with disabilities are laughable.
- Persons with disabilities are aggressive.
- Persons with disabilities are burdens or outcasts.
- Persons with disabilities are nonsexual.
- Persons with disabilities are unproductive and incapable of fully participating in everyday life.

Our studies of disability and disability experiences in Ghana confirm some of these stereotypes. From our research, these stereotypes did not only come from members of the society who were distant from persons with disabilities but also from direct relatives of persons with disabilities and sometimes from persons with disabilities themselves, who had internalized those stereotypes. For instance, the conception of disability as a tragedy and, therefore, persons with disabilities as objects of pity was common in many Ghanaian societies. One family member recounts how people in their community consoled them upon the occurrence of a disability in their family:

> *Actually, for people to visit and commiserate with us, people were visiting and saying oh, sorry for your trials, sorry for your trials.*

Literature suggests that the tragedy model of disability, which perceives disability in the manner of the above quote, contributes to the preservation of other "harmful stereotypes and misconceptions about PWDs" (Retief & Letšosa, 2018, p. 6).

There was also belief across a section of society that persons with speech and hearing impairments lack patience or are difficult to relate with. For example, a family member had this to say about his daughter with hearing impairment:

> *It is very hard to handle people with hearing impairments, so sometimes; I have to be patient with her if she does something. Otherwise, I encounter a lot of problems because of her inability to hear and speak.*

This quote affirms the stereotype that some persons with disabilities are aggressive. Moreso, the parent comes across as though it is because of his daughter's lack of verbal communication ability that she is "difficult" to relate with. There is no recourse to the fact that negative attitudes from society, including the family's inability to develop an effective means of communication with their daughter, could be the reasons for constant misunderstandings and the resulting frustrations for their daughter. In essence, the attitude from his daughter's environment rather than the disability should be targeted as the source of his daughter's behavior. The quote below confirms our position that the reactions of persons with hearing and/or speech impairments are due to attitudinal factors emanating from society.

> *To me, because I know she is my blood, I don't find it very difficult [to relate with her] but within the community, they find it very difficult. So, because of that, when she was growing up to about 18 years of age, whenever she went out, she always came home with different types of problems. She has stopped the aggressive response when people behave untoward to her. . . . Now she has come to terms with the fact that that is her nature so now whenever people do things to her, she does not take it harshly again. Now she is mature and understands things when they happen.*

Clearly, the above quote suggests that the source of the aggression is "society's untoward behaviour" towards her. However, the expectation, as can be inferred from the quote, is for the victim, who is at no fault, to change in order to conform rather than for the perpetrators to reform and desist from their discriminatory attitudes. From the quote, the young lady with speech and hearing impairments had to learn to cope with, and not react to, societal aggression toward her as the only means to live peaceably in this society. This could also mean she internalized the stereotype as being the aggressor and therefore would no longer respond to negative attitudes toward her. If the latter is the case, then we can expect that she will perpetually live in subjugation. As Foucault (1982) suggests, when power continually acts on a subject over time, the subject will end up conforming to the dictates of the power. This effectively would mean her loss of agency and self-determination within her society.

Similarly, persons with mental illness are stereotyped as aggressive or violent. A mother of an adult woman with mental illness narrates how this stereotype led to her struggles in helping her daughter when she traveled with her to another town:

> *. . . I begged a group of young men to help me lift her up. They told me they could not help me because the woman was very strong. Then I asked them, how is it possible that one woman will be stronger than all of you men put together? When I asked them this, they had a change of mind and decided to help me out. But when they wanted to touch her, she said they should stop. She got up by herself and boarded the bus.*

It is evident that stereotypes like these have consequences for the care of persons with mental illness. This explains why most persons with mental illness in Ghana experience extreme neglect and marginalization

(Mfoafo-M'Carthy & Grischow, 2022; Moasun & Mfoafo-M'Carthy, 2021).

We have also seen from the list of stereotypes above that across Africa, there is a misconception that persons with disabilities are unproductive and incapable of full participation in society. In an affirmation to the existence of this stereotype in the Ghana context is the quote from a family member of a person with vision disability:

> *. . . because once you become blind, you can no longer move about, work, go to the farm, trade and do so many other things that will enable you to earn money to take good care of the children. So, it made us sad. It is not like an abled [able-bodied] person who can go around, do what they want and at the end of the day, the children will feel happy. But now that my sister is blind, and we are women and her husband is dead, all hopes were lost.*

From the above excerpt, and as is common with the medical model of disability (Devlin & Pothier, 2006; Hosking, 2008; Sullivan, 2011), we can see an attempt to lay blame on the blindness as the reason the person in question is no longer able to work and earn a living. There is an absolute loss of sight on the fact that with an enabling environment (Crabtree, 2013; Oliver, 2004), the woman who has become blind could still work to earn a living for herself and her family.

Extant literature suggests that mental illness is one of the most stereotyped and misconceived disabling conditions in most parts of Africa. In addition to the belief that persons with mental illness are aggressive or violent, as discussed earlier, another pervasive misconception of mental illness is the belief that the condition is incurable (Moasun & Mfoafo-M'Carthy, 2021; Sottie et al., 2018). While our studies of disability in Ghana confirm the persistence of these stereotypes of mental illness, we also found the tendency for society to perceive persons with mental illness as lacking personhood, what a mother to an adult with disability referred to as not being "proper persons."

> *There are times when she sits there and you come to meet her, you will think she is a proper person. But when it arouses her [she experiences an episode], she will pace around screaming and sometimes laughing.*

Again, it is important to reiterate that the misconception of a person as lacking (adequate) personhood is the starting point for society to begin to withdraw from and isolate the individuals. This consequently results in neglect for many persons with mental illnesses in Ghana and other parts of Africa (Mfoafo-M'Carthy & Grischow, 2022; Mfoafo-M'Carthy& Sossou, 2017).

Myths

Like stereotypes, myths can be significant sources of misconceptions, stigma, and marginalization for persons with disabilities. A myth is defined by Bolle et al. (2022) as "a symbolic narrative, usually of unknown origin and at least partly traditional, that ostensibly relates actual events and that is especially associated with religious belief" (para. 1). It is important to clarify that, because myths largely emanate from belief systems, some of the beliefs about disability discussed earlier fit as myths. The purpose of this section is to emphasize these beliefs and provide more context to the ways that they operate to marginalize and exclude persons with disabilities.

The following myths gleaned from disability literature in Africa explain the reasons a child might be born with a deformity or impairment (Agbenyega, 2003; Haihambo & Lightfoot, 2010; Setume, 2016):

- The mother slept with multiple partners during her pregnancy.
- The family tried to get rich by using traditional doctors but failed to carry out the traditional doctors' instructions to the letter.
- A jealous rival who wanted the husband of the (expectant) mother bewitched the family.
- The woman had sex with a man who is not the father of the baby while pregnant.
- The woman was mean to animals such as crocodiles or snakes while pregnant.
- Because of witchcraft.
- Because of punishment from God.
- Because of a curse by ancestors.

Our observations and analysis of data collected on disability in Ghana confirm the existence of similar myths. Agbenyega (2003), for instance, describes the situation where some children with disabilities are referred to as snake children because of the myth that their mothers were mean to snakes, which used their supernatural powers to punish them with these children. On the other hand, there are those children who are referred to as river children because of similar beliefs in the powers of river animals like crocodiles to punish mothers with children with disabilities for being mean to them. In our studies, we found, for example, that there was a belief that non-hereditary conditions such as hearing and speech impairments could be passed on from the mother to the child. Thus, society feared that if a woman has hearing and/or speech impairments, she will give birth to children who would have hearing and/or speech impairments. This myth is evident in the quote below:

> *Before I married my wife [who had hearing and speech impairments], it was one man who impregnated her and abandoned her and the pregnancy. Simply because people said that when you marry a deaf woman, the deaf woman will give birth to children who will also be deaf. . . . Even when she gave birth, people came and looked at the baby and started giving different interpretations, they said the child is not crying so she is deaf. Some pointed out that there was something under the child's tongue, so the child is deaf. . . . When I took her to the hospital, they [doctors] assessed her and said there was nothing wrong with her.*

With such a belief, it is no surprise that the first man who impregnated the woman abandoned her at such a crucial time in her life. The myth is a source of fear for potential suitors of women with hearing and speech impairments. Another implication of this myth is the fact that there does not seem to be anything wrong with dating and having sex with women with disabilities, but men would not like to have children with them because they will bring forth children with disabilities. The women, then, are only desirable for sex but not for partnerships that lead to childbirth.

The myth that persons with disabilities and their families are cursed was also evident in our studies of the Ghanaian context. For example, one woman whose sister was blind and who was also gradually losing her sight shared that

> *Sometimes some people say our family is cursed. They do not understand why both my sister and I could be suffering from eye problems at the same time . . . they say we are cursed and do not want to have anything to do with us.*

As indicated earlier, myths can be sources of social isolation and neglect for persons with disabilities. By assuming that the family is cursed, there is an indirect message sent across to avoid relating positively with the family and to avoid the wrath of the spirit responsible for cursing them. Baker and Imafidon (2020) suggest that myths can lead to a misdirection of treatment and care for persons with disabilities. For example, conditions in children that may be treatable by medical professionals when caught early might be referred to traditional healers for spiritual attention, which might degenerate into serious impairments. Again, some African disability scholars have shown that there are instances where disability myths have resulted in the murder of children with disabilities (Agbenyega, 2003; Denham et al., 2010; Moasun, 2019).

One interesting myth that was shared by a participant from the northern part of Ghana is the belief that it is only chiefs or affluent people who can marry women with disabilities. The participant's words were as follows:

*[A] lot of people said that it is chiefs who marry deaf women. If you are not a chief, you cannot marry a deaf woman. . . . It is the chief who can marry a disabled person [*sic*], and nothing will happen . . . but if you are a young boy and you marry a deaf woman you will die or face misfortunes. This is practice is common among the Dagombas*, the Nanumbas*, the Gonja* and even the Mamprusi*.*[4] *It is the chief who marries disabled women [*sic*].*

While, on the one hand, such a practice may be an opportunity for women with disabilities to be provided with care and support, on the other hand, it can be a source of tokenism and patronage for women with disabilities. It smacks of marriage out of charity or pity, not out of love. We are aware of the implications of the charity or tragedy model for persons with disabilities (see Retief & Letšosa, 2018). It also means that in the event that the chief is not willing or capable of marrying all women with disabilities within his jurisdiction, the women might end up never getting married. Thus, besides the fact that men would usually not want to marry women with disabilities, the situations of women are complicated by the fact that even if men were willing to marry them, the fear of offending the chief would deter them from doing so. In effect, this myth has the potential to subject women with disabilities to the risks of physical and emotional neglect. On the other hand, if a chief marries a woman with disability as a result of pity and not out of love, she is likely to face emotional abuse and neglect.

CONCLUSION

Disability and disability experiences occur within specific cultural spaces, and this fact ought not to be overlooked. These spaces are bound and regulated by culture and belief systems, which in turn influence societal understanding of disability and attitudes toward persons with disabilities. In this chapter, we have demonstrated how culture, through language, belief systems, stereotypes, and myths can define and affect the lives of persons with disabilities in specific ways. We have made the case in respect of language that African disability language is evolving and that the lack of an established disability language has implications for how disability is known and understood. We have also made a case in this chapter through some of the examples shared that the fledgling disability language in Africa means there are terms and referents to impairments and disability that are mainly derogatory and have the tendency of leading to negative attitudes and behaviors toward persons with disabilities. We then proceeded to identify some proverbs in the Ghanaian context that portray disability and persons with disabilities negatively and therefore have the tendency to influence the mistreatment of persons with disabilities, including their abuse, neglect, or marginalization. The chapter also discussed Ghanaian indigenous beliefs about disability, most of which proceed from a moral or religious models' perspective. The discussion of the beliefs about disability set the tone for us to delve into specific stereotypes and myths and ways that they may contribute to stigma and marginalization of persons with disabilities. It is our hope that this chapter has both enriched your understanding of disability and engendered your desire to want to know more about the place of culture in people's experiences of disability in Ghana.

NOTES

1. This is the language spoken by Bikpakpaam (corrupted and now known as Konkomba people).
2. Much of the information contained in this and the previous paragraph has been published in a book chapter by Moasun (2023).
3. Personhood refers to conditions that a human being must meet to be considered a person.
4. * These are major ethnic groups in the northern part of Ghana.

Chapter 3

Religion, Spirituality, and Mental Illness in Ghana

INTRODUCTION

Religion and spirituality play a significant role in understanding mental health in Africa. According to Mbiti (1969), "the African is notoriously religious" (p. 1). Others have used terms like "incurably religious" to describe the mindset of Africans. According to Mbiti, religion is an "ontological phenomenon" which addresses the nature of existence. He argues that religion plays an important role in the daily lives of the African; thus, it permeates every thought process of Africans. In Ghana, for instance, exchange of pleasantries in the form of greetings is often accompanied by invoking the name of God. For instance, asking a person how they are doing would generate a response like "by the grace of God, I am doing well."

Stigma toward mental illness in Ghana is often steeped in socio-religious underpinnings. To better understand this phenomenon, one must understand Ghana's religious-spiritual context, specifically as it relates to the causation and treatment of mental illnesses. Ghana is a highly religious nation, and research has shown that over 95 percent of Ghanaians identify with a religion. This belief system explains conceptualizations of mental illness as punishment for sinful acts, moral depravity, or demon possession (Alhassan & Ridwan, 2021; Dako-Gyeke & Donkor, 2018; Gyamfi et al., 2022; Kpobi & Swartz, 2018; Lamptey, 2019; Yendork et al., 2018).

Mental health, according to the World Health Organization (WHO), is defined as a state of well-being in which every individual realizes his or her own potential.[1] That is, they can cope with the normal stresses of life, work productively and fruitfully, and be able to contribute to their community (2014). Mental disorders are generally characterized by a combination of abnormal thoughts, perceptions, emotions, behavior, and relationships with others (WHO, 2017). Mental illness is a major health condition that affects individuals, families, and communities in both the developed and developing worlds. The World Health Organization (2013) estimates that one-quarter of the world's population will likely experience mental illness in their lifetime. Mental illness affects people of different backgrounds and cultures, irrespective of age, gender, race, education, religion, or socioeconomic status (Regehr & Glancy, 2021). Individuals diagnosed with mental illness find themselves stigmatized by family, society, and the community at large. A large majority of individuals with the illness find themselves discriminated against due to society's perception of mental illness (Regehr & Glancy, 2021).

It is therefore understandable that the conceptualizations of mental illness and its origins are based in religion and spirituality. Findings from numerous studies examining how mental illness is understood in Ghana have reported that mental illnesses are often attributed to religious or supernatural causes, such as demon possession, witchcraft, or repercussions for sinful acts (Edwards, 2014; Gyamfi et al., 2021; Kpobi & Swartz, 2018; Mfoafo-M'Carthy & Grischow, 2021; Yendork et al., 2018). For example, in an article exploring beliefs about and treatment of mental disorders among Muslim traditional healers, Kpobi and Swartz (2018) reported that belief in the existence of spirits and entities that can influence behavior is common within Islam. Thus, many Muslim healers explained the atypical or disruptive behaviors that often accompany mental disorders as a possession of the evil spirit, "Jinn," or an evil eye, "Nazr," that originates within the afflicted individuals.

In this chapter, the authors will explore religion and spirituality in the Ghanaian milieu and how this affects the well-being of individuals diagnosed with mental illness. Efforts will be made to address causation, treatment, and challenges associated with being diagnosed with mental illness in a religious country like Ghana and the collaboration between Western psychiatry and faith-based treatment.

CULTURE, DISABILITY, AND MENTAL ILLNESS

Ghanaians hold peculiar beliefs about supernatural possession and witchcraft causing psychosocial disability or mental illness (Acheampong et al., 2020; Lamptey, 2019; Alhassan & Ridwan, 2021; Avoke, 2002; Dako-Gyeke & Donkor, 2018). Culturally, many Ghanaians believe that "the natural world is partly physical but mostly spiritual and that occurrences in the spiritual world can manifest in the physical world" (Opare-Henaku & Utsey, 2017, p. 503). This belief is reinforced by many Christian clergy, especially Pentecostals, who "lean more towards a diabolical explanatory model of mental health than a biomedical perspective. As such, church leaders and congregants attribute mental illness to demonic intrusion into human affairs" (Asamoah et al., 2014, pp. 601, 604). When combined, traditional beliefs and Christian spirituality—often held simultaneously—lead Ghanaians to ascribe mental illness to three types of spiritual causes: sorcery by humans, punishment by ancestral or evil spirits, and interventions by a Supreme Being (Bonsu & Yendork, 2019; Yendork et al., 2016). These beliefs can be manifested in assumptions about specific conditions ascribed to mental illness, such as epilepsy, which Ghanaians commonly ascribe to demonic possession and which are believed to be contagious (Acheampong et. al., 2020; Agbenyega, 2002; Dako-Gyeke & Donkor, 2018).

These spiritually rooted beliefs have real consequences. For example, children with any form of mental illness or any form of disability are subjected to physical abuse in efforts to expel the demons believed to be possessing them (Kassah et al., 2012). Moral explanations for mental illness have been cited in Islamic and Judeo-Christian religions, the two most widely practiced religions in Ghana. This is a potential explanation for widespread belief in the connection between religion, morality, and mental health (Amedome & Bedi, 2018). In an article theorizing different models of psychosocial disability, Alhassan & Ridwan (2021) introduced the moral/religious model as one of several that shape the views that many hold about individuals with mental illness. This model assumes that mental illnesses are the result of crimes or sins that have been committed either by the individual, or their relatives, or their ancestors. There are still communities in Ghana that ascribe to this model, particularly among those that frequently practice religion and magic (Karna, 2002).

Poor spirituality or potential wrongdoing can contribute to the existing stigma surrounding mental disorders, as it suggests that those afflicted are responsible for the decline of their health. This often leaves them vulnerable to mistreatment, isolation, and discrimination by their families and communities. Unlike Western cultures that consider mental illness and disability as individual afflictions, Ghana's collectivist culture often conceptualizes mental disorders in children as a failure of the child's family and community (Alhassan & Ridwan, 2021). In a study examining the portrayal of children in Northern Ghana, Alhassan & Ridwan (2021) argued that it is the duty of the parents to raise children into productive citizens as they will eventually be tasked with the care of their aging parents. Thus, children with severe forms of mental disorders who cannot meet these expectations are often met with abuse and neglect at the hands of their families. Moreover, misconceptions about those with disabilities being able to spread their misfortune result in further isolation from one's community (Acheampong et al., 2020). Therefore, an overreliance on religious or supernatural explanations can exacerbate the stigma and misconception surrounding the origins of mental health challenges. The mistreatment of persons with mental illness who have sought treatment is also a common occurrence among traditional, faith-based treatment pathways. Due to the commonly held belief that mental disorders are the result of supernatural phenomena, many individuals prefer to also seek treatment based in spiritual practices (Kpobi & Swartz, 2018). However, faith-based healing centers in Ghana are under increasing scrutiny due to poor living conditions and inhumane treatment of their patients.

> In Ghana, the belief and practice of witchcraft and its relation to mental illnesses and seeking of mental health treatments from native doctors/traditional healings and spiritual/prayer camps healers are common and these traditional healers are regarded as part of the wider cultural belief systems. (Mfoafo-M'Carthy & Sossou, 2017, pp. 131–132)

Due to cultural beliefs and myths, mental illnesses are perceived as curses from the gods for evil deeds committed by individuals with the illness or from family misdeeds either in the past or present. Also, Twumasi (1979), in his seminal research in Ghana, identified two main medical systems: the Western and traditional systems of practice. According to him, the traditional systems of practice consisted of traditional healers, often known as herbalists, who mostly used herbs for healing, and cult healers who dealt with witchcraft and disasters in social life pertaining to their followers, and the leaders of syncretic or spiritual churches who used prayers and other religious ritualization to heal members of their faith. He further asserts that the common essential element in traditional medicine is the utilization of magico-religious acts and symbols in diagnosis and therapeutics (Twumasi, 1979).

According to Read et al. (2009), traditional healers and pastors of Pentecostal churches interact with a large proportion of individuals with mental disorders in Ghana. Ofori-Atta et al. (2010) argue that many individuals in need of mental health treatment do not seek psychiatric services but rather seek care from informal community mental health services such as traditional and faith healers. For many Ghanaians, the first point of contact with treatment is in the form of faith-based treatment centers or prayer camps, which often treat mental illness through reading of scripture, fasting, and prayer (Lambert et al., 2020; Yendork et al., 2018). This form of treatment continues to remain popular, despite receiving increasing criticism for human rights violations. For example, incidents of chaining, poor living conditions, starvation, and sexual and physical abuse have been cited by residents as common occurrences (Edwards, 2014; Lambert et al., 2020).

Potential explanations for this trend require a deeper understanding of Ghana's cultural context and current mental health sector, as beliefs and attitudes toward mental illness and disability are influenced by unique sociocultural perspectives. Attributing mental disorders to poor character or sinful acts can also leave those struggling with mental disorders more vulnerable to stigma, leading to severe mistreatment and exclusion from their communities (Acheampong et al., 2020; Dako-Gyeke & Donkor, 2018; Lamptey, 2019). However, faith-based treatment currently plays a significant role in the existing treatment gap in Ghana's mental health sector, due to increased accessibility and cultural congruence between healers and patients (Kpobi & Swartz, 2018; Lambert, 2020; Read, 2019).

Despite Ghana's mental health law passed in 2012, which banned the use of inhumane practices such as flogging and shackling, the lack of regulation of traditional treatment centers and prayer camps has allowed for these practices to continue (Human Rights Watch [HRW], 2019). In an article detailing the treatment of mental health patients residing in prayer camps, Edwards (2014) reported instances of overcrowding, poor hygiene, withholding of food, and inadequate shelter at eight prayer camps across the country. Additionally, several survivors have recounted experiences of physical and sexual abuse, forced starvation, chaining, and sleep deprivation. Another study also found that 30 percent of residents treated in a faith-based healing center had experienced some form of maltreatment and reported higher post-traumatic stress symptoms (Lambert et al., 2020). However, Lambert et al. (2020) also found that, despite being subjected to harmful practices while residing in the treatment center, many patients return to such facilities to seek further treatment. Notwithstanding the potential for exposure to mistreatment, this form of treatment remains popular, suggesting that mental health treatment is firmly rooted in religious and spiritual practices.

One of the most well-known Ghanaians who had to endure treatment through traditional healers and Pentecostal faith pastors is Doris Appiah Danquah. The following vignette illustrates her story very clearly:

> Ms. Doris Appiah Danquah attended one of the premier high schools in Ghana, Achimota School in Accra. Due to her excellent academic performance, she was eventually admitted to the Medical School at the University of Ghana. However, she had to eventually drop out of Ghana Medical School due to bouts of depression which made it difficult for her to focus on her studies. For a period of approximately 22 years, Ms. Appiah Danquah was moved from one place to another while being drugged, stigmatized, chained, and beaten at spiritual camps and at fetish shrines. At one point, she was made to understand that her mother had cursed her and caused her to be mentally ill.
>
> Also, she was told that her condition was a result of not serving God well, and so she would never recover. In one incident, a group of children who knew her bought her food, but then threw the plate away after she had finished eating due to their belief that her illness was contagious. Ms. Appiah Danquah eventually enrolled in a nursing program because she could not go back to study medicine. Upon graduation, the difficulty she experienced in attempting to find work in her field could be attributed to stigma and discrimination. Ms. Appiah Danquah

is currently an influential advocate for the rights of the mentally ill in Ghana. (Mfoafo-M'Carthy & Sossou, 2017, pp. 130–131)

As we shall discover, Ms. Appiah Danquah's experience is very common in Ghana. Our participants' narratives confirm that stigma and discrimination toward mental illness in Ghana tend to be rooted in religion and spirituality. However, we found that institutionalized religion, while imposing negative stereotypes and beliefs about mental illness, also provides a sense and place of refuge, offering a coping mechanism and source of resilience in the face of stigma and discrimination. The remainder of the chapter takes up these themes, privileging the voices of our respondents.

PERCEPTION OF RELIGION AND SPIRITUALITY AMONG INDIVIDUALS WITH MENTAL ILLNESS

Most participants reported negative life consequences connected to the idea that mental illnesses are caused by demon possession, sin, curses, or other harmful spiritual forces beyond human control or imposed by others with connections to the spirit world. These accusations were made by family members, friends, and church congregations. For example, after admitting to consuming alcohol and taking marijuana, one patient said that a fellow church member attributed the mental illness to sin and insisted that he "needed to ask for forgiveness." Another believed that they had been under a curse "that the enemy has used against me to destroy my life." In another case, the participant's symptoms began with restless sleep, and, believing that the cause was spiritual, his father took him to a church for help from the pastors.

At the church, he had another episode that led to a fall on the way back from the restroom, after which he seemed to become physically challenged ("my back raised a little") and psychologically troubled. The pastor scolded the participant for leaving the group to use the restroom, saying that the urgent need to urinate "could be because of the prayers." The pastors then searched for a spiritual diagnosis.

So, the pastors surrounded me and prayed for me. After that, they didn't bring me back home, they took me to one of my sisters in Accra. . . . They sat me down to talk to me. The main thing is that, they asked me lots of questions about what led to the experiences I was having. I also told them the root cause of the thing. . . . The thing was that I didn't know whether it was a vision or a dream: that was what I was experiencing.

This passage reveals the intense pressure that can be brought to bear on mentally ill church members who suffer from mental illness, as families, pastors, and other congregants repeatedly confront individuals in the search for spiritual roots of the mental illnesses. The pressure can be amplified if individuals also lead lifestyles deemed immoral by the church. In one case, the church became involved during a participant's first episode with mental illness, which the pastor attributed to the sins of marijuana and alcohol consumption:

> *I took some of the alcohol and chewed some of the weed. So, I started experiencing changes in my behavior. That is how come I came to this facility. . . . Before we even went to the hospital at Akrokerri (town in Ghana), someone came to pray for me with olive oil. So, I narrated to (the pastor) that I took in weed and alomo bitters (locally brewed alcohol beverage). So, he asked me why I did that, and I told him I didn't know why. So, he told me that I have sinned, so I needed to ask for forgiveness of sins.*

The participant believed that excess alcohol and marijuana use contributed to their mental illness. However, the church went a step further and perceived the ultimate cause as sin, which presumably might be addressed through admitting the sin and asking for forgiveness. The participant did not reveal whether the church attempted to heal them through confession and absolution. If there was an attempt, it did not succeed, and the individual ultimately was institutionalized. But rather than being sent to a hospital simply as a patient suffering from a mental illness, the church labeled them a sinner as well. This story and the other narratives presented above show that institutionalized religion plays a significant role in the imposition of stigma against Ghanaians with mental illness.

Perhaps more important than imposed attributions of mental illness to spiritual causes, our data revealed that many participants (most of whom were Christians) had internalized this belief themselves. We heard many stories from respondents who believed personally that their condition resulted from evil spirits. For example, a participant told us that

> *the doctors couldn't diagnose the illness. So, we perceived it was a spiritual illness. For so many months, I couldn't eat and I grew very lean. So, my relatives referred to me as "the living dead." Those in this institution are people suffering from spiritual attack.*

One might expect the participant to have reacted negatively to relatives referring to him as "the living dead" and conjuring up images of the undead who should be avoided out of fear. However, this participant appeared to accept that description and believed that the other institutionalized patients had suffered similar spiritual attacks. Similarly, another participant told us:

The thing started when I was in my room. I was praying in my room. All of a sudden, I became afraid in the room, so I took to my heels with my Bible and mentioning the name of Jesus. So, that day, I didn't sleep in my room. I slept over my brother's place. . . . I was brought here (to the hospital . . . because of the spirit that entered my room.

This recollection is very similar to the participant discussed above who was not sure if their mental illness resulted from a vision or a dream. But in this case, the individual conveyed a much greater sense of an actual spiritual presence in their room. The result was the same, however: institutionalization in a psychiatric hospital. As such, not only do the narratives offer insights into the extent to which mentally ill Ghanaians attribute the causes of their illness or condition to spiritual forces, which are external to their persons; they also demonstrate that individuals who are institutionalized can carry the added stigma of being labeled sinners or spiritually possessed.

In the narratives presented above, our respondents reported that spiritual beliefs and treatments had serious negative consequences, including physical abuse and a lack of effective care. However, many participants also told us that their religious beliefs also offered coping mechanisms. Most of our participants are devout Christians, and many of them accept their conditions as God's will and believe that God will help them to persevere and recover. The following discussion present a grassroots narrative on this topic, organized into three themes: belief in God, accepting mental illness as God's destiny, and depending on God for strength in the face of stigma and discrimination.

Belief in God

Despite being stigmatized by the church, many of our respondents also coped through their belief in God. The belief that mental illness was not the end of life, and that God had a purpose for their lives, was a good motivator in helping them deal with their situations. This belief gave the respondents the strength to live and to hope for better circumstances. "*Well, I came to understand that that is the way God created me*," said one participant with a physical disability. They added:

So, I have to take it like that. . . . Everyone was created differently by God, with different behaviors and attitudes. Some people can treat you as if you are part of their family. . . . God has lifted me. Now everyone sees me, that I can also walk. I feel happiness deep inside.

The idea that God created everyone, including persons with disabilities, helped other participants as well, as illustrated by two further statements:

It makes me feel that God does what he wants, and he knows what he's doing. And maybe he wants me on direct path, so I need someone to support me. . . . The Bible. I use the word of God.

*I believe it is God who created the disabled [*sic*] that is why I feel it is not good to be tagged as disabled [*sic*]. Christianity has truly changed peoples' perception about disability.*

Another told us that God's presence helped them to cope with their pain.

Sometimes if you want to into the public, if it is not because you know God is on your side you will not even wish to go out. I already have a lot of pain in me, and I am not willing to add more pain to it. So, I just let it go. God is there for me.

Accepting their disabilities as God's will also motivated some of our participants to pursue education and knowledge-based work rather than give up on their futures because of the limitations imposed by their disabilities.

What I intended doing was that since I wasn't strong enough to engaged in what the abled person does, I would use the knowledge that God gave me to work.

I sat down and asked myself that "what's my purpose on this earth" I therefore decided to give my life to Christ at the age of 12 years and education.

At their core, these statements reveal the resilience among Ghanaians with disabilities that can come from belief in God. In a country like Ghana, where religion is dominant, it is not surprising to see that most of the participants relied on a deity for hope and strength. Their belief in God gives them the assurance that the future could get better; it also gives them the strength to believe in themselves and the hope for a better life.

Leaving Everything to God and Accepting Mental Illness as Destiny

There can be a downside, however, to attributing disabilities to God's will. A majority of our participants adopted the "I give it to God" stance by accepting their situations as a matter of destiny. However, for some of them, instead of acting toward improving their situations—such as confronting the system with regarding to mistreatments against them—they tended to resort to religious faith and therefore leave everything to God (Allah) to handle it on their behalf. Several statements illustrated this feeling of resignation very clearly:

Well, as human, it reduces your status in society. But in my situation, there is nothing much that I can do but to give it all to God. I give it to God because in this condition, I cannot do anything, so I must be patient and give it to God.

I read myself and I read how all the situation is moving and I see that all is from God. Because it is God who created me, and it is God who gave me this thing [the disability]. It is only that some people don't think far. That is why they are doing all these things to me. So, I give everything to Almighty. (Peace Man, person with physical disability)

Masha Allah! I just give everything to God. Because with God, everything is possible. Masha Allah! . . . I felt worried at first but now I feel better because I have seen that by the grace of Allah, to have survived, I thank God. I don't think it to be a problem for me.

Other Muslim participants also left their fate to Allah, referring to the Holy Quran for inspiration through meditation and prayer for God's protection.

Frankly speaking, I use the Quran. Every day I use the Quran. I pray every time that God should provide everything for me and protect me from any bad thing. As for prayers, I don't joke with it. Everything I do, I use prayers to back me.

Others simply accepted their condition as their destiny.

Once we are human beings, we keep ourselves silent in that order. What can I do? I won't kill myself because of that one. So, I just live my life. I must take it like that. Everybody and the way we are born to live in this world.

Others simply will not do anything at all about it but leave it to God, as evident in the following:

What can I do? I only exercise patience and leave it to God. I feel like it is the gift that God has given to me. Everyone born into this world is given a gift by God and I feel that it is my gift from God, and I have to cope with it. She is a human being and it was my choice to marry her, so I have to cope with all the challenges that come with it and live with her. I think that I have always managed it. I try to be quiet and to allow the will of God to take its course and to live peacefully with everybody. I cannot leave this town. I cannot also create my own village and go to live there and if I go to a different town at all, maybe it will be worst, so I have to remain patient and live here like that.

Like I said, it pains a lot, but I have nothing to do about it. So, we just leave it to God almighty. Because he knows where he wants to put them or how He wants them to be.

For example, a participant told us that

> *certain conditions brought us here. For me, I thank God for whatever happened because, maybe, my husband to-be wanted me to learn something from here. And my dad also wanted me to learn something from here.*

Another participant put it this way:

> *Oh, but it's God's plan. He made me go through that to make me what I am now. If I didn't go through that, I would not be the man I am. So, I don't look back, I don't regret it. But I wish I could have gone about things differently. . . . So, if anything, what happened to me now has matured me. I believe it's in God's plan, so I don't worry.*

Family members also turned to faith in God to help them cope with and accept their children's disabilities.

> *Honestly, I know my wife is a deaf but I knew what I was going in for when I married her and so I cope with her. I feel that oh, my wife is a deaf and everything is gifted by God. I have married her and there is no problem with me and our children, so I like that.*

> *I always think that it is by God's own design that my mother became blind. I know that people will always call her a blind person. So, I leave it to God. . . . My mother's sickness is the will of God. So, what will I do?*

These narratives paint a different picture of spirituality and disability than the negative accounts presented above of stigma produced by accusations of sinfulness or spiritual possession. In our participants' narratives, the relationship between spirituality and disability is therefore complicated and cannot be reduced to simple pronouncements.

Simply put, in many cases, spirituality had a positive impact and contributed to resilience in the face of stigma. Most importantly, beyond simply leaving things to God, religious beliefs helped participants to accept and handle their conditions.

> *They sometimes call me an illiterate and even tell me my head is not well shaped. You know wisdom and knowledge, it is God that gives it. But I do not care because, I know God created us in his own image. So, if even the shape of my head is not good, it is God's handiworks. It pains me when they call me an illiterate but what will I do? There is nothing I can do. . . . Thank God, all the challenges I face within my society I am able to handle it. It is not by my might nor by wisdom but the grace of God.*

> *When (my mother) told me we were going to church, I was very happy. I like going to church a lot and do not joke with church service. I can recite Psalm 27, 35, and 91 without looking into the Bible. Thank God, all the challenges I face within my society I am able to handle it. "It is not by my might nor by wisdom but by the grace of God"* [in the Christian Bible Book of Zechariah 4:6].

This participant quoted a verse from the Bible to argue that she is an overcomer despite the challenges of the devil, as she put it.

Other participants believed that God had intervened or would intervene to help them. For example, one participant said that God protected him from attempting suicide:

> *Sometimes too, I look for poison to take so that it will end my life. . . . I had a niece (and) something told me to go to her. So, I boarded a car to her place, but you see, God is so wonderful that some of the things he does, we cannot understand. I know her house, I have been taken there before. I took a car that I was going there to talk to her in private to give me some medication (poison) I can take to end my life, so that I will be free. Do you know that, that very night, I took a car to the place, but I couldn't locate the house, so I had to return home.*

In the following quote, the participant believed that God sent an aunt to protect her and her children:

> *I came here again not long ago, and I met (my aunt). It is just a small illness that the enemy has used against me to destroy my life and I have left my children at home. But I know God himself will protect them for me. . . . From the time I came here, my relatives have not visited me yet but I trust that aunty Gladys will come. Because she is the one God has sent to come and help me . . . I want to be discharged so that I can go home. I want to regain my memory so that I can go back to school. The way Job was faithful to God and he delivered him, I know he will deliver me too.*

These stories illustrate that, in addition to their negative consequences, spiritual beliefs offer a coping mechanism, helping people to accept their conditions as God's will and giving them hope that God will protect them or maybe even provide a cure.

Dependence on God

Another coping method was depending on God. This was a form of strength to accept their mental condition and its responsibilities. Existence of a belief system was a way to deal with the inexplicable occurrences that they had to deal with in taking care of their condition.

> *Anything that happened with my brother, only God helped us through it all. It was only God. . . . After taking care of my brother till now that he can speak well and walk, I thank God. . . . God really helped us for all of us.*
>
> *That one was painful but not always because I know his condition. Even though he is disabled* [sic]*, it isn't by his own choice. It is the will of God.*
>
> *When he got sick . . . there is a saying that "the disease has already happened" so I could not keep him indoors. So, you only had to leave everything to God. Whatever God will do, we accept it.*
>
> *I was only praying to God about this situation, I was coping by praying. . . . No, I wasn't coping with anything physically but just prayers with God.*
>
> *I only depend on my Christian faith. Disability has been something from the olden days. The bible even lets us know that "not all that glitters is gold" hence he is the partner God has given to me and I accept.*

Most of the participants expressed faith in God as a way of coping with the situation. Their faith in God served as a source of comfort. It helped them to better understand the situation they were dealing.

SUPPORT FROM INSTITUTIONALIZED RELIGION

The church proved very essential in supporting some of the respondents deal with their situation. The church, as a community, provided them with people who were willing to accept them. Aside from being accepted in the church, some were given roles in the church that enhanced their status in the church. These were some of the views shared.

> *I also contribute a lot to church. I am accepted at church. They know I am disabled* [sic] *but they know that I have good intentions, they know that I am a good person.*
>
> *Members from my church help to provide encouragement and show that they care about me. . . . I open up to people who are God fearing as they believe the disability does not define who I am but rather an accident that has happened along the line as they get closer to me.*
>
> *The inspiration came from the pastor's advice from church which prompted me. According to the pastor's advice disability does not mean inability, moreover disability does not mean destroyed.*
>
> *Yes, for instance my church has been very supportive emotionally due to that I have become an evangelist.*
>
> *Oh, for where I worship, they encourage me, even what I feel I can't do they will encourage me that I can do:*

> *. . . from the time we came (to the town) till now (the members of our former church) are fine with us. And where Papa [*the reverend minister*] was ordained, they are also fine with us. When we close from (our current) church the members great her and ask her how she is doing, if we are not able to take her along the same thing they will say (our daughter) didn't come, how is she?*

Beyond encouragement and home visits, churches also provided concrete support and services. In two cases of parents with young children with disabilities, pastors and congregations offered gifts or financial support, as seen above, and one respondent also told us that "*occasionally the pastor comes here to give me communion . . . and sometimes gives me GH₵10* (equivalent to 2 USD at the time)." In other cases, respondents received support and encouragement from their congregations and visits from their pastors.

Other participants recounted stories of being taken by family members to pastors who prayed over them, believing that the prayers might lead to a cure. For example, one participant stated:

> *After the prayers, I became so aggressive and uncontrollable, so they had to send me to the health Centre. . . . I was later sent to a certain woman at Obuasi (town in Ghana) for prayers. I stayed there for a while and later transferred to Kumasi (city in Ghana) for prayers again.*

Also, through the church, some of the participants shared that they were elevated to positions that improved their statuses in their communities. They were given the voice and the opportunity to speak on matters and to be leaders of groups in the church. These activities instill in them confidence and the ability to achieve their goals.

Coping mechanisms and resilience were some of the more surprising findings of the study. Their existence should not, however, be used as an excuse for inaction. Though religion offers a place of refuge, it is also part of the larger problem of stigma, which in turn lies at the root of many of our participants' negative experiences. Thus, the participants sharing their stories provide a sense of empowerment through engaging in discourse that helps destigmatize mental illness. Beyond this, it offers the hope that publicizing the lived experiences of mental illness encourages the Ghanaian citizenry to respond out of a sense of duty, necessity, and community. Part of that response should be the provision of resources, including personnel, to treat individuals diagnosed with mental illness.

CONCLUSION

Our participants' narratives revealed important themes connected to the lived experiences of individuals diagnosed with mental illness. First, religion and spirituality are centrally important to their lives in two distinct ways: as an explanation of their illness and as an approach to treatment. Most of our participants are members of Christian communities, many of whom ascribe mental illness to demonic and supernatural forces that can be mitigated by faith in God. As a result, religion is not only part of the problem but also the preferred place of refuge. The latter phenomenon has not been reported widely in the literature. Instead, researchers have focused on treatment methods used by the churches, especially faith healing and/or exorcism (e.g., Asamoah et al., 2014; Osafo, 2016; Yendork et al., 2016). The role of Christian faith as a coping mechanism, even in the absence of treatment, deserves further research.

Despite the influence of religion and spirituality in Ghana, we argue that mental health care in Ghana could potentially see improvements through collaboration between biomedical psychiatric treatment and faith-based treatment. Although instances of mistreatment have been cited in traditional healing centers, religion can serve as a protective factor for those with mental illness and should not be eradicated entirely (Amedome & Bedi, 2018; Gyimah et al., 2022). For example, Amedome and Bedi (2018) found that those who identify as religious experience less psychological distress, higher life satisfaction, and higher achievement of goals. Furthermore, findings have also shown that prayer camp residents have had comforting and healing experiences during their stay (Lambert et al., 2020). As previously mentioned, Ghana is a highly religious country with unique religious-cultural perspectives that shape conceptualizations of mental illness. Additionally, faith healers have been considered important resources, able to deliver services that are considerate of traditional belief systems. Thus, researchers have suggested increased partnership between biomedical treatment and faith-based healing as a more appropriate method of improving the quality and accessibility of mental healthcare (Hanlon & Alem, 2020; Kpobi & Swartz, 2018).

In a study exploring the effectiveness of a collaborative shared care model between faith healers and healthcare workers in Nigeria and Ghana, Hanlon & Alemu (2020) reported that clinical and functional outcomes were significantly improved among patients in the shared care group. Additionally, harmful practices decreased significantly over time among this group. This is particularly promising, as researchers have expressed concerns over collaboration due to the unethical practices that are commonly implemented in faith-based healing centers and prayer camps (Lambert et al., 2020). Read (2019) further supports notions of collaboration as a means to reduce harmful practices and argues that if access to psychiatry increased, bio-medical psychiatric treatment could replace inhumane treatment such as chaining. Thus, there is hope that partnership between formal and informal treatment could provide safer, more accessible, and culturally relevant mental health services. As one example of a possible way forward, we encountered an example of a doctor who incorporated spiritual beliefs into a biomedical intervention. During their interview, a participant told us:

> *I was hearing voices but couldn't see the people who were talking. So, when I came here, the doctor said I was suffering from schizophrenia. He said because I wasn't in contact with reality that was why I was hearing voices which is spiritual. . . . I believed that it was a spiritual thing. Because I don't learn too much, and I do not smoke marijuana I believed it was spiritual. . . . The doctor then told me he will give me medication so that I become well again, I was very happy because I don't like spiritual things.*

We realize the physician's approach buttresses the importance of not solely focusing on spirituality but the need to explore biomedical interventions as well. In any case, it is a very interesting choice and one that raises important questions about the practical relationship between spiritual beliefs and Western medicine in Ghana.

NOTE

1. Portions of this chapter are based on Mfoafo-M'Carthy and Grischow (2017 and 2021).

Chapter 4

Stigma, Discrimination, and Impact on Individuals with Disabilities

INTRODUCTION

This chapter explores the experiences of persons with disability with regard to stigma and discrimination and its impact on their day-to-day lives. Disability is a global phenomenon, affecting the lives of diverse communities and populations around the world. The World Bank estimates that more than one billion people worldwide experience some form of disability, including between 80 and 300 million in Africa (African Studies Centre, Leiden, 2023). Unfortunately, individuals with disabilities are faced with untold challenges on a regular basis. These challenges include the need to be accepted by society and the fight against stigma and discrimination. Disability includes varying forms of impairments—visual, hearing, physical impairments, angular kyphosis, and epilepsy, to name a few. Generally, diseases, wars, accidents, and poor health services, as well as ,medical errors have been shown to be major causes of disabilities across the world. In some circumstances, being born with disabilities is often attributed to several factors (Denham, 2017). In Ghana, most people attribute disability to the machinations of witchcraft, curses, and demonic activities, which leads to stigmatization and discrimination. Beyond generalized discrimination, having a diagnosis of disabilities can create difficulties in obtaining and maintaining employment (Angermeyer et al., 2014; Brohan et al., 2011; Gary, 2005; Lyons et al., 2009), obtaining adequate housing (Corrigan, 2004), obtaining health care, and creating "affiliation with a diverse group of people" (Corrigan & Watson, 2002, p. 16). Being employed has been shown to help reduce self-stigma (Broham et al., 2011). Yet due to all these forms of discrimination, individuals diagnosed with disabilities often feel alienated and socially withdraw (Ritsher & Phelan, 2004).

DISABILITY STIGMA AND DISCRIMINATION IN THE SCHOLARLY LITERATURE

Stigma and discrimination against individuals with disabilities stem from many sources, but in African societies they are often associated with spirituality, which includes the belief that disabilities are as a result of curses, demonic possession, or in some cases the "sins of the fathers being visited upon family members" (Mfoafo-M'Carthy & Sossou, 2017). In Ghana, stigma tends to drive families to abandon relatives with disabilities in spiritual camps where they suffer abuse and neglect (Liu, 2016; Read et al., 2009) or in hospitals without family visits or contact of any kind (Barke et al., 2011). As a result, individuals with disabilities are neglected and rendered powerless and voiceless.

Goffman (1963) described stigma as human "attributes that are discrediting" (p. 3) and noted that stigma emanates from a myriad of factors, which include devaluation, separation, discrimination, labeling, and stereotyping in the context of imbalances in societal power (Link & Phelan, 2001). In Ghana, the impact of stigma is documented in the literature (Mfoafo-M'Carthy & Grischow, 2021; Mfoafo-M'Carthy & Sossou, 2017). For example, the delay in seeking help (Abdulmalik et al., 2019) reduces the quality of life for persons with disabilities and their families (Degnan et al., 2021). Caregivers of persons with disabilities experience high levels of stress, shame and blame, anxiety and depression, avoidance of social contact, and reduced self-worth (Hermann et al., 2018). It is noted that culture and religion play a significant role in contributing to stigma and discrimination of persons with disability (Spittel et al., 2018). Stigma is a barrier to the management and access to support and treatment for persons with disability. It is often associated with ignorance, that is, lack of knowledge, prejudice, and negative consequences.

Recent literature posits four main locations of stigma in Ghana: the workplace, the community, among family members, and by healthcare providers. At the workplace, studies have shown that employers have the tendency not to hire individuals diagnosed with disabilities, instead preferring those who are able-bodied (Adu et al., 2021; Bonsu & Yendork, 2019). In other studies, it has been stated that workers reported feeling uncomfortable and not wanting to be around individuals with disabilities because they are compelled to witness derogatory comments (Dako-Gyeke & Asumang, 2013; Gyamfi & Hegadoren, 2017). At the community level, studies showed that friends, neighbors, and strangers fear individuals with disabilities. As a result, persons with disabilities are shunned as community members refuse to live close to them, and families and prospective in-laws object to proposed marriages (Barke et al., 2011; Sottie et al., 2018). Individuals with disabilities have also reported being shunned or ostracized by community organizations and even religious institutions (Thornicroft & Kassam, 2007).

Studies show that individuals with disabilities are often mistreated, at times violently, mocked by family members, and at times denied access to their children and hidden away in their homes so they would not know they exist (Barke et al., 2011; Bonsu & Yendork, 2019; Gyamfi & Hegadoren, 2017). It has also been reported that healthcare providers tend to stigmatize and mistreat patients by denying them much-needed support or sometimes forcibly detaining and/or physically abusing them (Bonsu & Yendork, 2019; Gyamfi & Hegadoren, 2017; Thornicroft & Kassam, 2007). In Ghana, there is the underlying belief that at every level disabilities are caused by supernatural forces. One study, for example, reported that many of the informants attributed disabilities to "evil spirits, sorcery and witchcraft" (Read, 2009, p. 7). In some cases, these beliefs—combined with a lack of medical treatment facilities—push family members into taking relatives with disabilities to traditional fetish shrines or Christian prayer camps to be treated spiritually for their condition (Read, 2016).

Society's perception of stigma and discrimination is observed from the analysis of the data from the participants' perspective. For some, the fear of stigma and discrimination from society dominated their minds upon the realization that they had a disability. For others, it was the fear that they would be neglected and thus suffer (Liu, 2016; Read et al., 2009). While others entertained the fear of how their dependents, especially their children, would survive or be cared for. The fear of neglect and suffering dominated the initial concerns of some of these individuals when they initially realized that they had disabilities. Perhaps, this speaks to the evidence of neglect of persons with disabilities in their communities. Various participants with diverse disabilities had the following to say concerning their initial fears upon realizing they had a disability. With respect to the fear of stigma, two participants shared the following thoughts:

> *Like when I completed JHS and I was able to pass, and when the placement came, I got a school. But after I got the school, my worry was that I am now going to mix with other people. Those I don't even know. I didn't even know their lives. So, my problem was whether they were going to be distancing themselves from me because I have a hunchback. That was one problem. I was thinking whether if I get there, they will be distancing themselves from me because of my having a disability.*

I worried about how I will be getting support. Because as at that time, I didn't know who will support me and who will not support me. You see, when things like this happens to you at the beginning everyone will promise you help but not all will come to your aid in the end. So, it was a big worry to me.

These statements speak to the issue of social exclusion resulting from stigma and the extent to which the fear of stigma-produced exclusion made participants hesitate to attend school. Even before experiencing stigma first-hand, our participants felt its weight and considered withdrawing from an important social setting based on the possibility of maltreatment.

One of the factors behind fears of stigma is rooted in the impact of Ghanaian culture on attitudes and assumptions toward the causes of disability. Findings have shown that while many Ghanaians acknowledge trauma and environmental stressors in producing disabilities, it is also common in Ghana to identify curses and spirituality (including witchcraft) as significant or even central factors as well (Yendork et al., 2018). Research has shown that even healthcare providers with more extensive training and education often perpetuate misconceptions about disabilities, and their causes, impacting the quality of care of their patients (Acheampong et al., 2020; Barke et al., 2011). Acheampong et al. (2020) found that healthcare providers periodically perceived those with disabilities as difficult to work with and communicate with and low in self-esteem. These misconceptions are likely to contribute to the breakdown of the provider-patient relationship, negatively affecting subsequent treatment and further discouraging individuals from seeking treatment.

The current state of Ghana's health sector also offers a partial explanation for why faith-based healing remains the preferred method of treatment for individuals with disabilities. This suggests that many Ghanaians struggling with disabilities are unable to access biomedical treatment, and professionals remain inaccessible for the majority of those with disabilities. They reported constantly being reminded of their illnesses through derogatory remarks and name-calling by family members, friends, and strangers in the community. Some referred more explicitly to the problem of stigma in their daily lives. Others were institutionalized, abused physically by family members and strangers, and banished from public spaces. These experiences harmed our participants deeply at a personal level. They felt fear and shame, which led them to hide their conditions from the public and withdraw from their communities.

As efforts are made to implement additional disability services, they should be centered around collaboration between healers and formal healthcare systems (Hanlon & Alem, 2020; Read, 2019). There should be an effort to ensure collaboration that can provide appropriate improvements to healthcare and education that are of Ghanaian worldviews and perspectives.

CAUSATION OF DISABILITY AND MENTAL ILLNESS IN GHANA

The literature attributes causation of disability to a myriad of factors, and this was captured in the data collected from the participants. In Ghana, the cause of disability is attributed to numerous factors. Explanations for the causes of disabilities worldwide abound in the literature (Edwards, 2014; Gyamfi et al., 2021; Kpobi & Swartz, 2018; Mfoafo-M'Carthy & Grischow, 2021; Yendork et al., 2018). Generally, diseases, wars, accidents, poor health services, and medical errors have been considered to be major causes of disabilities across the world. From the study's findings, even though some participants indicated their lack of knowledge of the causes of their disabilities, those who were aware of the causes mentioned, among other things, accidents, diseases or sicknesses, and medical errors as the sources of their disabilities. There were others who assigned their disabilities to spiritual factors.

Accidents

Among our participants who became disabled through accidents, two were work-related, while a third was related to road accidents.

> *I used to be a farmer until I was able to buy a grinding mill. It was through the grinding mill business that I became blind. I was at the grinding mill and a metal substance which was in the item I was grinding splashed into my eyes.*

> *I went to the farm, I was starting a new yam farm, you know we, we are farmers here. When we farm, after the gemination of the yams, we cut support sticks for the yam vines. So, I was on top of a tree, trimming branches for yam support. Before I realized, I fell and I was even rushed to . . ., they took me to the hospital and then I realized that I am not able to walk again.*

Although accidents are common and obvious biomedical causes of disability in Ghana, many Ghanaians attribute the accidents themselves to spiritual forces, including witchcraft or curses, through which enemies maim or destroy people by disabling them. The socioeconomic harm produced by the belief that disabled Ghanaians have been cursed can be far-reaching. In the case of the participant quoted above, the status as a cursed person affected his farming business to the point where he had to give up farming and resort to either begging or depending on others for assistance.

Medical Illness or Disease as Causes of Disabilities

Many of our participants knew that illnesses caused their disabilities. For example, two individuals whose conditions deteriorated as a result of an illness shared their respective experiences as follows:

I got the disability through sickness. I fell sick and when I became well, I could not walk again. (Peace Man, person with physical disability)

My mother told me that I was perfectly fine until I had measles. When I recovered from the sickness, I could not hear and speak again.

At least two participants also shared that they had received injections to prevent poliomyelitis, which ironically led to their disability. In the quote below, this participant indicates vaccination in this respect to have led to his current condition.

Hmmm, I feel sorry for myself because the thing happened when I was in primary two. There were, you see, in Ghana here, you know, the health officers will be going around that they are injecting children to prevent polio. So, it was through that injection that I got my disability.

This participant expressed sorrow due to the state in which he finds himself. Though this is as a result of medical malpractice or error, individuals with similar conditions find themselves marginalized and unable to play an active role in society.

Spiritual Causes of Disability

Even though most participants believed that their disabilities had biomedical explanations, most of them also expressed beliefs in spiritual causes. There were those who believed that their disabilities were caused by clandestine acts of human beings against them.

I have been hearing from my parents that it was through humanity. I mean . . . human beings used spiritual means to get me into this state. It was through some family disagreement. There was some misunderstanding in the family. Before my mother got married to my father, there was one of my father's sisters who was not in favour of the marriage. She insisted that my father should not marry my mother. So, when my father did not listen and married my mother, my father's sister caused me to develop the hunchback. So, this thing was caused by my father's sister. She did this to me. (Famous)

This passage speaks to the belief that disabilities can result from curses against individuals, oftentimes arising from disputes and conflict. However, in these cases, almost all participants believed that God was ultimately responsible for their disabilities. They believed that if it were not the will of God, their present would have been different. For example, even though one participant blamed his aunt for having cursed them spiritually to cause his disability, he still believes that it was the will of God. He said subsequently to the above quote:

> *Hmmm (giggles). Although I have said my aunt caused my disability, it doesn't mean I do not believe that God was behind all this. I will say everything happens because it is God's will. So, I believe that God has designed it that it may be through this disability that I will get to reach my destiny.*

Some informants also invoked God's will even when they knew for certain the physical causes of their disabilities. For example, two participants who became disabled through an accident and a faulty injection both told us that God was pulling the strings:

> *But you see, no one goes to beg for the disability. It is given by God. God gives everybody his share of things. God gives everything.*

> *They say it is God; he wants you like that and he put you into that situation so you shouldn't bother so much about it.*

The mindset of most of the persons with disability is to associate their condition with the supernatural, and this could be in the form of curses or acts of God. A typical example is participant Famous' assertion about his condition, which he attributes to his aunt. Despite their challenges, persons with disability continue to express confidence in God. They see Him as the creator who is in charge of the universe and thus have the belief that it is God who grants permission for the curses to prevail.

Understanding Stigma and Discrimination

We define stigma as "the social judgment, degradation, or devaluation of individuals" because of their disabilities or because they have been labeled as such by others (Abdullah & Brown, 2011, p. 936). Stigma generally occurs in situations where the non-stigmatized population has more power than the stigmatized group (Mfoafo-M'Carthy et al., 2016; Schulze, 2009). Our data indicated that it is difficult to present persons with disabilities experiences of stigma separately from their experiences of discrimination because of the intricately connected nature of the two phenomena. This is not uncommon because stigma, which is intangible, is made manifest by discriminatory practices, which are more perceptible. Therefore, this section is practically an extension of the presentation on the stigma experiences of persons with disabilities. In many cases, stigma leads to discrimination against individuals diagnosed with disability, which can take several forms, including "withholding help, avoidance, coercive treatment, and segregated institutions" (Corrigan & Watson, 2002, p. 17).

Though most of the participants could not directly define the concept of stigma, they exhibited their understanding of the concept by describing how it is perceived. From the analysis, it appears that participants' understanding of stigma centered on people distancing themselves from an individual as being unworthy or undesirable to be interacted with, as stated by some of the participants. This understanding cut across the responses of many participants when asked to articulate their perception of the concept, as did, more significantly, the fact that people do not want to eat food or drink water from a common source with a person diagnosed with mental illness or a disability:

> *Erhm, stigma is when you are with people, like if this is a room for a disabled [*sic*] person and three or four abled people to share, and they do not like me to lie close to them. Or when we are supposed to drink water from a common pot, they will not like me to drink from the pot with them. Even if we are to roam (stroll together), they will not like me to be in their company.*

> *I understand that in our homes, community, people shy away from us. It is like a disease. When you talk to me or you touch me, it is like contagious. It will affect you too. So, in a meeting or gathering, stigma is when people don't want to come close to us because of our disabilities.*

These testimonies reveal that the fear of stigma and social exclusion, as expressed by the participants above who hesitated to attend school, is well founded.

Some of the participants also understood the phenomenon to mean treating some people as being less important or placing less value on them, as shown in the quotes below:

> *Stigma is just about, for example, in my family or among my friends or other relatives around me, sometimes, they don't value me, or they don't see me as anything or even a person. Because there are some things that I am supposed to be part of, but they are rejecting me because of my disability.*

> *It is like the society not recognizing that a disabled person [*sic*] is like them and so they disregard the disabled person [*sic*] and don't want to get closer to him/her because he has a disability. That is what is referred to as stigma.*

From the way these persons with disabilities characterized stigma, it is evident that members of their community predominantly view persons with disabilities from a position of inferiority, and as one of the participants put it, they behave toward persons with disabilities as if their disabilities were contagious. Hence, the tendency to avoid interacting with them or eating and drinking from the same sources as them.

Persons with disabilities shared their experiences of stigma within their respective societies that did not differ from their understanding of the phenomenon. From the analysis of the data, the experiences of stigma by persons with disabilities ranged from being treated as a person of less value and therefore not deserving the best of society. Others were given labels that replaced their names, while for most of the participants, their encounters with stigma were in respect to people not wanting to involve them in communal activities such as eating or drinking with them or involving them in social activities, even to the extent that people would walk away when they get close to them. Just as distancing or refusal to associate with people dominated their explanations of their understanding of stigma, persons with disabilities' experience of the phenomenon of stigma was similarly dominated by people shunning their company or sharing items with them.

From the above narrative, we realize fear and ignorance serve as a contributing factor to the stigma associated with the condition of epilepsy and the subsequent neglect of the person with epilepsy. However, more deliberate instances of stigma could be inferred from the quotes below:

> *When I went to school with the condition, some people welcomed me, but others run away from me. I asked them why? They said, [pauses], some were having in mind that maybe because of family matters or my deeds or other things that I had this thing. Some people were thinking that maybe it was because I did some bad things. They did not understand why a car can have an accident and I was the only person having this kind of condition. I even approached somebody, and he told me the same thing. So, I told him that it is not from me. I didn't do anything [wrong]. Then they said then if it is not me then maybe it is from my family and then I said ok, that is their perception. People from, those from south (Southern Ghana), they were just running away from me. Even as I am talking to you, as I am in the university now, still, I still experience some of these things. Because for that, sometimes you will talk to them, but they refuse to understand you.*

This narrative reveals other issues worth mentioning here. First, there is a clear indication that irrespective of how one's disability came about, people are bound to assign spiritual reasons to it, and this is a major source of stigma toward persons with disabilities. Second, we observe that this experience took place on a university campus, which could suggest that stigma against persons with disabilities is perpetrated by persons, irrespective of their levels of education (Johnson, 1979). This highlights how stigma is ingrained in the mindset of the general population. This speaks to the fact that despite our level of education or exposure to knowledge, people are bound to discriminate and treat individuals with disability differently.

IMPACT OF STIGMA ON PERSONS WITH DISABILITIES

Disability stigma is widespread and perpetuated through many forms, most commonly expressed and experienced through social processes. Holder et al. (2019) identified social stigma as particularly pervasive because it is contingent upon the knowledge of social structures, which are quickly learned by most members of a social group. In many communities, disability is often associated with negative stereotypes of weak character and incompetence, among several other harmful assumptions (Holder et al., 2019). Additionally, these stereotypes, among others, suggest a level of personal accountability for one's disability, which is also demonstrated as an individual responsibility.

Exposure to public views of disability can also result in the internalization of stigmatizing attitudes. Self-stigma is another form of stigma characterized by negative self-judgment because those with disabilities recognize that they will be subject to prejudice and discrimination due to their mental illness (Corrigan, 2012). Like other forms of stigma, self-stigma can result in feelings of shame and embarassment (Holder, 2019). Thus, individuals with disabilities can learn to accept and identify with the public's negative perceptions. As negative stereotypes surrounding their existence within several communities, it is likely that many are vulnerable to the internalization of harmful stereotypes.

Labeling and Name-Calling

Stigma impacts persons with disabilities in numerous ways, and this affect their self-esteem. Participants shared instances of name calling and negative attitudes toward them. Some will ignore your name like my name is xx, and then they will be calling you cripple, cripple. Meanwhile cripple is not the name that my parents gave me.

People do refer to me by it [the disability] and I respond to it. In our dialect, they call it "gulgulana." So, some people do call me Gulgulana (the hunchback) and then I respond to it.

Persons with disability are often treated badly and, in some circumstances, as second-class citizens. Some are assigned derogatory names to make fun of their condition. This has resulted in many of them either giving up or having their self-esteem seriously impacted.

Denial of Right to Marry

Stigma is so culturally embedded in the psyche of most Ghanaians that some avoid marrying into families where there are individuals with disabilities or mental illness (Adebeyi, 2016). For some persons with disabilities, the stigma came from the individuals they had proposed love and marriage to. However, for others, the stigma stemmed from family members even in the face of their love partners accepting to marry them. Some of them shared their struggles to getting a partner to marry in the following narratives:

> *Actually, people behave badly towards me, even if I approach a woman. As at now I am not married. Because of my disability, if I approach a woman and she notice that I am a deaf, then the woman will reject me. I also have the right to marry but whenever I approach a woman, she will turn me down because I am a disabled* [sic]. *That makes me get worried about my life. Does it mean that if I am a disabled person* [sic], *I do not have right to marry? . . . I was interested in a lady who also loved me, and I went and paid the bride price. The woman was coming to me every day, and then one day the woman stopped coming suddenly. When I asked her why, she said it was because I am a deaf, she cannot marry me. I can remember that it pained me a lot. Since then, I have never had a woman in my life again.*
>
> *Yeah. When I was going to marry my wife, one of my neighbors went and told the father of my wife that as you are going to give this girl or this lady to this man, would he, or can he take care of her? Can he make her happy? Can he feed her? I don't think a disabled person* [sic] *can take care of your daughter. So, don't give your daughter to him. When I went to him, it was a story he gave to me and laughed and said people don't know. If you ask God and God told you that this thing cannot happen or this man cannot do this, then that is fine.*

In the above quote, we find that there are individuals who are supportive and vouch for persons with disabilities, like the father-in-law in the latter quote. Without the support of his father-in-law, he might have been in the same situation as the other participant in the former quote. It appears that their ability to take care of the financial needs of their future partners was the overt reason for the opposition or refusal of marriage to persons with disabilities. In some cultures, disability is akin to being deemed undesirable by family members. This is based on the stigma and the fact that families fear their children may not be well taken care of due to the condition of their partner.

Stereotypes as Unconscious Bias against Persons with Disabilities

Analysis of the data revealed that many of the cases of stigma were based on stereotypes that persons with disabilities were incapable of rising to the challenges of life like persons without disabilities. Thus, in some instances where persons with disabilities were stigmatized, especially by their family members, this was done without ill motives. In some of the instances, as evidenced in the quote below. In this quote, the participant's experience of stigma stemmed from acts of over-protection on the part of his parents.

Despite these actions constituting overprotection of persons with disabilities, they were stigmatizing and hurt the feelings of persons with disabilities:

> *Even in my house, my dad and my mum, there are some common things that if I want to go closer to, they warn me not to get closer. They think I am not capable. I cannot do it; I should go away because I am no longer like I used to be. So, I should go and sit for those who can do it to do it. So sometimes I will have it in mind to go. Sometimes when they have family gatherings or something like that, I don't know whether they forget about me or something like that. They won't consult me.*

Another participant shared an instance when he experienced emotional discomfort because of his wife's inadvertence:

> *Yes. Yes. Really, really, my wife! My wife (with emphasis) called me a disabled person [*sic*], what can I do? My wife told me this. You know my junior brother, our last born, I am taking care of him. He also told me the same thing. . . . Ok, it was one time, I spoke to her about the future of the children. I asked her, "these children, how are we going to take care of them?" And then she told me that you are a disabled man [*sic*]. What can you do? And I told her, through God, I can do something. Insha Allah!*

Such stereotypes do not just affect persons with disabilities in their homes but extend to their quest to secure employment, as shared by two participants in their experiences of the phenomenon:

> *I can remember once my uncle was the national youth employment coordinator in this district. That was in 2008. That was the year I completed my senior high education. So, when we completed and I was staying at home, I went to his office and greeted him and I wished he would employ me so that I could also be getting some little income to use to take care of myself. What he had to tell me was that the only vacancy left was teaching, and I couldn't teach because I could not stand and therefore, I couldn't copy notes on the board for the children.*
>
> *Let me use the public as an example. If there is a gathering and they want everybody to come or maybe they are distributing certain things or they are recruiting the youth into the Youth Employment modules, we have all picked forms before. But when you go for interviews, they will tell you they want only people who are abled. They will tell you that even people who are abled did not get recruited and you a disabled person [*sic*] think you can be recruited.*

It appears that these were more deliberate and purposeful compared to what happens with stereotypes in the families of persons with disabilities. The participant highlights discriminatory practices regarding persons with disability. Stigma and discrimination tend to be meted out to persons with disability for the fact that society perceive them differently. They are seen as fragile, imbecile, and unable to make any contributions to society.

IMPACT OF STIGMA AND DISCRIMINATION

Persons with disabilities shared that they experienced significant challenges because of their disabilities. Thus, stigmatization and discrimination had a significant impact on persons with disabilities. In many cases, this led to them anticipating being treated differently in various situations. Having to live with this fear of potentially being stigmatized and discriminated against is debilitating and impacts self-esteem, as expressed by two of our participants:

> *Actually, since I was diagnosed with this condition, I have been demoted. Let me say, I have not been able to achieve my dream. Because what I had planned to do for myself in the future, everything has totally changed.*

> *Things changed for me when I realised that I could not hear and speak. Because now I find it difficult relating with people because I lack hearing and speech.*

In addition to generalized feelings of hopelessness as expressed in these two quotations, our participants shared experiences of encountering various forms of mistreatment by their families, communities, and government agencies. These forms of mistreatment included stigma-driven disrespect and its resulting discriminatory treatment of persons with disabilities. There was also an instance of physical abuse, as narrated by one participant. In terms of stigma, the study explored the concept for participants' understanding and their experience of the phenomenon, as well as the subsequent effect that the experiences of stigma have had on them.

Experience of Disrespect

For some of the persons with disabilities, the stigma they faced resulted in disrespect for them by members of their families and communities, as evidenced in the following quotes:

> *At times I may be having some policy [ideas] to make myself and when I tell them, and they think they have some other place to go. They can just leave me and go. Because I have no power over them again to tell them what I want them to do. Because, at first when I fell from the tree and I had this accident, I told them that they should not abandon the farm. Because they don't have anything doing. They are not employed. Our job here is farming so don't leave the farm. They left the farm and all my yam seeds, and everything got rotten. So, imagine, if I did not have a disability, the farm would have been there up to now.*

Culturally, having a disability makes one "voiceless," as illustrated in this participant's experience. That is, despite one's level of intelligence or level of influence, having a disability changes society's perception of the individual.

The mere fact that the participant had a disability as a result of a fall meant he could not be respected and listened to. Despite the instructions that they should maintain the farm, they refused to adhere to the directive and, as a result, allowed the farmland to deteriorate.

Abuse and Neglect of Persons with Disabilities

Beyond their experience of stigma and discrimination as presented above, persons with disabilities also experienced incidents of abuse and neglect at various levels in society. However, incidences of abuse were quite minimal, as per the findings of this study. We can infer from their experiences of stigma and discrimination that most, if not all the participants, suffered some form of emotional and psychological abuse, as will be presented shortly under the effects of stigma and discrimination on persons with disabilities. With regards to physical abuse, only one participant shared an experience relating to physical abuse.

> *The way these people were treating me, it is like, they forgot that I was not like this before. It was a time that we were sitting together. We were just in a chatting mood and then somebody just got up and slapped me. Then I asked him why? He told me that I have too much mouth (talked too much/ was too vocal). So, I asked him, the time I was not like this, could you have done this to me? It was just painful. There, I started crying.*

Neglect was one form of mistreatment that almost all participants had encountered in one way or the other. Participants narrated their experiences with neglect at the family, community, and state levels. Findings showed that participants were more concerned about their physical needs than any other form of need; therefore, many of the instances of neglect expressed by participants were physical in nature. At the family level, the following are excerpts of some of the experiences shared by persons with disabilities.

> *My mother was a good carer. But as I am talking to you, she is not alive anymore. I was not feeling bad when she was alive. But due to certain reasons beyond our control, erh, unfortunately she passed away. Since then, I faced a lot. Erh we all beg the Almighty that He will take care of everything. Erh, anyway, my father is alive. But I didn't grow in the hands of my father. So, erh, he doesn't care about me. Because those he gave birth to after me, they are able, and they can go to farm. I didn't see any difficulties they face in life. So, I can use myself as an example for my colleagues, erh what do we call it? In other villages that also live the life that I have lived because they also face same challenges.*

> *In fact, since I got this problem, I do not get any form of support either social support or support in terms of resources. So, I was left alone. Anything at all that I want, nobody is willing to provide for me.*

To tell you the truth, I don't have anybody. I feed myself through the cobbler work that I do. I take care of all my needs through this. . . . I have family members. We are living in the same house. But they do not give me much help. The only help they give to me is, sometimes when they cook, they give me food to eat. Sometimes but not all the time.

Participants also shared stories that showed that they experienced neglect at the community level. Yet again, these stories were reminiscent of physical neglect as seen in the following quotes:

The community is not helping. They are not helping. . . . I don't know whether it is due to our situation here. Because here, you know we are all farmers, we are all handicaps I can say. . . . Ahaa! We are all in need.

I think people do not care so much about people who have mental illnesses in our communities. . . . Some of them are left to roam about. Well, I may also say some people do show concern for them. Why am I saying this? When a person becomes mentally ill and roams about the streets, they are unable to fend for themselves. It is individuals in the community that provides for them to feed. So, to that extent, I will say that some people are concerned and help them at least with food.

It is worth noting that the findings revealed very little about neglect at the community level. This might be because persons with disabilities viewed neglect only from the material perspective. Thus, as we note, especially from the quote from Baba's story, in an impoverished community where people struggle to fend for themselves, it will be unrealistic for persons with disabilities to expect any form of material support from their neighbors who themselves are struggling. Naday's expressions show, however, that despite the visible challenges, as shared by Baba, some community members do care for and support persons with disabilities.

One final source of disrespect is worth mentioning briefly. In addition to stigma and discrimination by families and communities, some participants also felt neglected by the Ghanaian government, especially due to the difficulty and inability to access public funds. For example, the government allocates 3 percent of its District Assembly Common Fund for disability projects. To access the fund, persons with disabilities are required to apply with specific plans to use the fund productively. While laudable on paper, in practice, many prospective applicants face major hurdles, and there is a sense that the fund is beyond their reach. For example, one participant told us:

I think the major challenge is the lack of support. We are not getting any form of support. Like the district assembly common fund, we are not getting it. But they said, it is mainly, mainly the 2% [3%] is for persons with disabilities. But when they pay it to the district coffers, before you go there, they will tell you that they are using it for different purposes. Even if they are to give you, like as I said I sew smocks, they will give me only GH₵200.00 and with this amount, it cannot buy the materials I need to sew two smocks.

Taken as a whole, the grassroots narratives from our participants reveal that culturally based stigma is a major problem for Ghanaians with disabilities, producing feelings of inadequacy and social isolation.

CONCLUSION

Sometimes the best suggestions for solutions to a problem are the ones given by those who experience the impact of the problem. Therefore, it was imperative that the study sourced from persons with disabilities and their caregivers, what they felt would be the best ways to address the challenges confronting them in terms of their experiences of disability stigma and discrimination. The main suggestions were made by persons with disabilities and their caregivers, including a call for education and sensitization and providing financial support to persons with disabilities. Some participants felt that the issues of stigma and discrimination they experienced were due to ignorance and lack of knowledge on disability issues. They argued that having a disability does not necessarily mean "inability." It is important for the general population to be educated and sensitized to the plight and needs of persons with disabilities. For instance, the teaching of sign language to the Ghanaian populace would allow for easy communication with persons with hearing and speech disabilities.

Aside from communication, participants believe that financial support from the government and NGOs would end their plight, as they deemed it as help that would open a lot of doors and opportunities for them. This will include education, skill training, and investing in business so they would be empowered and not dependent on family or the state.

Based on the participants feedback, we realized that society's perception of disability and mental illness affects the well-being of individuals with the illness. The data proves that stigma and discrimination are prevalent in every sphere of society as it negatively impact those with disabilities or illnesses. The participants shared about enduring pain due to the way they feel marginalized and ostracized by family and society as a whole. Some talked about entertaining thoughts of suicide due to the psychosocial effects of the illness on their well-being. This study brings to the fore the importance of embracing both traditional, religious, and medical approaches to treatment, support, and insights for individuals with disability. This will require the collective efforts of the Ghanaian government, NGOs, and civil society to find ways of dealing with this prevalent issue of stigma and discrimination toward persons with disabilities.

Chapter 5

Stigma, Discrimination, and Impact on Ghanaian Families

INTRODUCTION

Disability may be perceived as a problem at the individual level, as championed by the medical model (Hosking, 2008; Sullivan, 2011). This perception of disability has been heavily criticized for not considering the roles that external factors such as the social and built environment play in the construction of disability and disability experiences (Oliver, 1990; Union of the Physically Impaired Against Segregation [UPIAS], 1976). Similarly, solely locating disability as an individual problem fails to recognize and consider vicarious experiences of disability by persons close to individuals with disabilities, also known as affiliated stigma (Sightsavers, 2021).

In the Global South, family members and caregivers of persons with disabilities bear more than the physical care responsibilities of individuals with disabilities. In Ghana and other parts of Africa, families and other persons who provide direct care for persons with disabilities experience disability stigma, marginalization, exclusion, and sometimes abuse, merely because there exists a person with disability among them (Mfoafo-M'Carthy et al., 2020; Nukunya, 2003). These experiences are accentuated by dominant beliefs about disability and its sources, as discussed in more detail in chapters 2 and 3. Thus, while there is significant anecdotal evidence of vicarious experiences of stigma and discrimination against family members and caregivers of persons with disabilities, this topic has often failed to attract the attention of disability researchers in Africa and specifically in Ghana.

Literature on the topic suggests that in Africa, families and caregivers who cater for individuals with intellectual disabilities, for example, are subjected to significant levels of stigma and discrimination within their communities (Mkabile et al., 2021). The belief, for example, that some individuals use parts of the bodies of their (unborn) children to exchange for material wealth (Agbenyega, 2003; Mkabile et al., 2021) has been noted to contribute to negative perceptions of families with individuals with disabilities, particularly where such families are wealthy. These perceptions often result in negative attitudes toward such families and caregivers of persons with disabilities.

This chapter contributes to the extant literature on this almost neglected topic as we draw on empirical data gathered from across Ghana. The chapter is presented in three main sections. The first section discusses stigma and discrimination against family members and caregivers of persons with disabilities, including direct and indirect experiences of stigma and discrimination. The second section discusses the ramifications, stigma, and discrimination for family members and caregivers of persons with disabilities. The chapter concludes with a discussion of the various coping mechanisms family members and caregivers of persons with disabilities have adapted to absorb the impact of negative societal attitudes toward them as they continue to care for individuals with disabilities.

STIGMA AND DISCRIMINATION AGAINST FAMILY MEMBERS AND CAREGIVERS OF PERSONS WITH DISABILITY

Stigma and discrimination are real experiences faced by family members and those who provide care to persons with disabilities in Ghana and other Sub-Saharan African countries (Trani et al., 2020). Family members and caregivers of persons with disabilities have been noted to face social isolation, derogatory name-calling, and, in some cases, others refusing to marry from their families (Mkabile et al., 2021). Nukunya (2003), for instance, suggests that in many Ghanaian societies, prospective partners are scrutinized for the history of disability in their families. Where there is slight evidence of a history of disability dating centuries back, marriages are declined, and sometimes existing marriages may be annulled. Mfoafo-M'Carthy et al. (2020) suggest that the stigma and social exclusions experienced by family members and caregivers of persons with disabilities often result in some levels of frustration and burnout that have negative consequences for their well-being and that of the individuals under their care.

The Britannica Dictionary defines stigma as a set of negative and often unfair beliefs that a society or group of people have about something. On the other hand, Manulife (2014) defines the concept as a stereotype that leads a dominant group to perceive a vulnerable group of people as unacceptably different. Stigma often engenders discrimination, which is defined by the Oxford Language Dictionary as the "unjust prejudicial treatment of different categories of people, especially on the grounds of ethnicity, age, sex, or disability." Stigma and discrimination, though different phenomena, often work together to negatively impact a person or group of people's experiences. The two phenomena are such that the unfair beliefs that constitute stigma feed into and influence discriminatory attitudes and behaviors toward those who are negatively impacted by them. Thus, stigma underlies and influences discrimination. Due to the intricate relationship between the two phenomena, this chapter discusses their cumulative manifestation on the families and caregivers of persons with disabilities rather than their unique manifestations. Results from our studies across Ghana suggest that family members and caregivers of persons with disabilities experienced direct and indirect stigma and discrimination because of their relationships with persons with disabilities.

FAMILY MEMBERS' DIRECT EXPERIENCES OF STIGMA AND DISCRIMINATION

Direct stigma and discrimination refer to instances where stereotypes and discriminatory practices were targeted directly at family members and caregivers. Family members and caregivers' experiences of direct stigma and discrimination included social exclusions, labeling or name-calling, and, in specific instances, facing difficulties finding marriage partners or maintaining existing marriages.

Social Exclusion and Loss of Friends

Mkabile et al. (2021) suggest, and as we have observed in chapter 2 of this book, that in African cultures, negative reactions to disabilities are moderated by beliefs and taboos about disability. These beliefs engender negative attitudes and behaviors toward persons with disabilities (Devlieger, 2015). However, evidence from our studies shows that family members and caregivers of persons with disabilities equally fall victim to such negative attitudes, including social exclusion and loss of existing friends, leading to isolation. The tendency for friends and community members to distance themselves from a family member or caregiver because of the occurrence of disability in their families is quite profound in Ghanaian societies. For example, a young lady from the northern part of Ghana whose older brother has a mental illness shared her frustrations with the reactions of friends and extended family in the following words:

> *At first, I had a lot of friends. But just because of him [her brother with mental illness], sometime when they come to the house and see him, they will just stop coming to you and a whole lot. Just because of him, a lot of family brothers*

[distant cousins] and sisters don't come here. Sometimes when they come around, they just stand far away and greet.

It is worth noting that while this participant experienced social exclusion due to her brother's mental illness, she sold food at the village market in the evenings and had members of her community patronizing her food, as observed by one of the authors of this book. Hence, it might be important to put in context, that while people may not necessarily relate to her in a social context, she still had some members of her community engaging in economic activities with her. This experience is peculiar in some sense, as often, communities tend to shun the wares of individuals due to stigma (Geurt & Komabu-Pomeyie, 2016).

Having a person with disability in the family has often also resulted in backbiting, in addition to the shunning of the companies of family members. For instance, a woman shared her family's experiences as follows:

People are talking a lot about us, about our blindness. . . . Sometimes, we hear people saying bad things and others saying it is God's gift, others speak ill about us. Some people move away from us the moment you come to sit by them.

It is important to clarify in the case of the above participant that even though she granted the interview as a family member who gave care to a sister with vision disability, she was partially blind herself, and therefore any stigmatizing attitude toward her could be as a result of either her own disability or that of her sister or because of both. The experiences of this family could be accentuated by multiple members having similar disabilities because of the belief in intergenerational curses or that supernatural sources of the disability can extend the same to other members of the society who render help to people who have been cursed by the gods (Devlieger, 2015; Moasun, 2023). Thus, some of the exclusionary attitudes of society may simply be as a result of the fear of incurring the wrath of the gods should they positively associate with individuals with disabilities and their families (Moasun, 2023).

Labeling and Name-Calling

Labeling or name-calling another stigmatizing act that family members experienced by virtue of their relationships with persons with disabilities. Some of the name-callings were direct and aggressive, such as the following:

[I]f I am playing with others and a misunderstanding occurs, they tend to insult me such as a child of disabled woman [sic] *or the family of disabled people* [sic]*.*

While some family members experience aggressive labels like the above, there were instances where others, such as those below, experienced subtle name-calling.

> *My close friends were still coming to me, and we maintained a good relationship except that right from that moment, they stopped calling me by name and started calling me deaf's brother. That became the nickname that automatically replaced my name. instead of calling me by my given name, that is how they now call me.*
>
> *As for that one, several times. Naturally, we women sometimes go to fetch water or firewood in groups. But some of them, instead of calling me by my name they will just say, "hey bruku's*[1] *mother, wait for me so we can go together!!"*

Even though it appears in the above instances that name-calling was made lightly by community members, the participants did not take it lightly. Yet, the taken-for-granted nature of these acts appears to be deep-seated and difficult for the affected persons to deal with.

From the excerpts, it is apparent that the family members involved continued to maintain social relationships, unlike in situations where some experienced social exclusion and therefore isolation. However, these relationships, as we can infer from the expressions of the participants, could not be considered healthy. Such name-calling with an inadvertent impact on the victims is what some would refer to as micro-aggression (Sue, n.d.; Sue et al., 2007). Thus, while people label and call family members names, such as in the instance of the above quotes, with probably no negative intentions, their effects are no less negatively impactful on victims than those negative attitudes exhibited on purpose (Sue, n.d.). Trani et al. (2020) suggest that labeling is a critical recipe for discrimination against vulnerable social groups, such as those with disabilities and their families.

MARRIAGE-RELATED STIGMA AND DISCRIMINATION

Evidence pertains in Ghanaian disability literature to the effect that, due to stigma, members of families of persons with disabilities may struggle to find partners to marry because of the existence of a person with a disability in their families. Literature has it that families of prospective marriage partners would research the history of disability in the other family dating back to centuries (Attafuah, 2000; Green, 2003; Kassah, 2008; Nukunya, 2003). If historical evidence of the existence of disability in a family can present such significant impediments for family members to find partners to marry, we can only imagine what the situation is like for families within which there are currently individuals with disabilities. Our studies confirm this reality, as evident in the excerpt below:

> *I had a lady friend whom I planned to marry but her family members said the way my brother is, it is likely that when she marries me and gives birth, her children may inherit those things [disabilities]. So, they have the perception that if your family is having a member with the disability, when you marry into such a family, it is likely you will give birth and you will also have a child like that. . . . When they were saying those things, the lady decided that our marriage cannot work.*

While there was the case that persons from families that had members with disabilities were stigmatized and could not find marriage partners, there was the reverse, where individuals who defied the odds and married persons with disabilities faced stigma and discrimination from members of their communities. For instance, a man who was married to a woman with hearing and speech impairments shared his experience when he proposed to marry his wife:

> *When I first approached her, people said all sorts of things to me. They said a young man like me should not want to marry a deaf woman. People made fun of me. I heard so many things from the community, but it was my choice. So, upon all the mockery, I kept quiet and married her.*

Another man who got married to a woman with similar disabilities as the above's wife shared his experience as follows:

> *I will say that it is not easy to marry a deaf person simply because before you enter into the marriage, there are a lot of problems you face within the community and even among family members. . . . So, finally when I married her, I had to leave her at her mother's house . . . Even now, she is still in her mother's house because I don't want problems.*

In the case of the latter quote, the couple has been married for more than two and a half decades, and at the time of writing this chapter, their first child has graduated from a university in Ghana. However, the age-old stigma that comes with disability has prevented the wife from moving into her husband's home. Thus, it is almost as though the wife was being hidden from the sight of the husband's family, both for her own safety and that of her husband.

FAMILY MEMBERS AND CAREGIVERS' EXPERIENCES OF INDIRECT STIGMA AND DISCRIMINATION

By indirect stigma and discrimination, we are referring to family members and caregivers witnessing stereotypes and discriminatory practices directed at their relatives with disabilities. While these behaviors and attitudes are directed at individuals with disabilities, they have the potential to impact relatives and caregivers emotionally and psychologically. Like Green (2003) suggests in the case of maternal stress, the familial and emotional bonds that family and caregivers have with persons with disabilities mean they tend to experience and feel the impact of stigma and discrimination against their relatives with disabilities in similar ways as the victims themselves do. This is particularly the case when such negative behaviors are exhibited in the presence of family members and caregivers. It is for this reason that we deem it important to discuss some of the experiences of such indirect stigma and discrimination as shared by family members and caregivers of persons with disabilities across Ghana.

WITNESSING THE DISRESPECT FOR THE PERSONHOOD OF RELATIVES WITH DISABILITIES

In every society, there are standards set for human beings to meet in order to be considered persons (Dennett, 1976; Evnine, 2008). While we are unable to delve deeper into the concept of personhood, we are cognizant of the fact that some of these standards can be too high and unrealistic for some human beings to meet. For example, in certain societies, persons who are unable to speak, those with mental health conditions, among others, were deemed to lack personhood (Dennett, 1976; Evnine, 2008; Taylor, 1985). In Ghana, in addition to such bodily and physiological conditions, the willingness and ability to materially help others are integral to the definition of personhood (Moasun, 2019).

In many ways, persons with disabilities besides bodily impairments are mostly impoverished and are unable to provide help to others as expected by society (Moasun, 2023). This significantly affects their personhood and, therefore, the tendency for people in society to disrespect and accord them lesser status. When relatives of persons with disabilities observe incidents of disrespect for the personhood of their relatives with disabilities, they are emotionally and psychologically impacted (Green, 2003). Our research reveals significant levels of discomfort among family members and relatives when they observe incidents of disrespect for their relatives with disabilities. For example, a husband shared his experience observing society's reaction to his wife's blindness and the disrespect and abuse she had to endure in the following words:

> *[S]ometimes people talk to her in a negative way. Some people will say, look at the way your eyes are flowing with liquid, you should stay away from people. Sometimes she comes home crying and complaining. Because of her eyes, when*

she cooks, others will not eat it except me, her children and my children. Others around will not eat her food because they say her eyes drip with water.

In another instance, a mother of a woman with a mental illness expressed misgivings about her daughter's experience at a prayer camp in the following words:

It was at a prayer camp that a girl insulted her during prayers. Everyone was praying and she was also praying in her own way. Then this young lady heard her pray and burst into loud laughter, telling her friends to observe how my daughter is praying. Then the people at the camp quickly rebuked the young lady. They asked her if she was God to listen to other persons' prayers. I was offended and asked her whether she felt we were there to exhibit our beauty?

It is refreshing to note in the above example that there was some element of support for the person with a disability involved, as the abusive act was immediately condemned. This act of condemning the negative act could be a source of comfort for the mother, who, from the quote, was obviously distraught witnessing it.

In a related example, another participant shared that his sister, who had trained as a dressmaker, could not get patrons for her services because of stigma. In this example, there are implications for the brother to experience negative emotional impacts, but he also continued to bear financial responsibility for the well-being of his sister even after investing into her apprenticeship.

[A]s at now, like I said she has the skills all right but because of the stigma, they will not give their materials to her to sew dresses for them. And due to that she cannot get any money to even replace the machine when it gets spoiled and then I continue to provide for her.

The tendency for persons with disabilities to enroll in apprenticeship and train to acquire a skill is very high in Ghana. However, in many instances, when they acquire the skills, the stigma that comes with their disabilities does not permit them to move out of their economic dependence. Even as they are ready to render services to their communities with their skills, members of the community would not buy these services due to stigma (Geurt & Komabu-Pomeyie, 2016; Moasun, 2019).

WITNESSING THE LABELING AND NAME-CALLING OF RELATIVES WITH DISABILITIES

We have already shared the direct experiences of family members and caregivers with respect to labeling and name-calling. This section presents evidence of family members' observation of labeling and name-calling of their relatives with disabilities. As argued earlier, it is our firm belief that the outcome of whether an individual is directly labeled and name-called or observes similar negative attitudes toward his or her relative with disability may be felt the same way. Earlier in this chapter, we presented the experience in regard to a family member being labeled as "bruku's mother." In the excerpts below, we present the experiences of participants witnessing their relatives being labeled with negative referents:

> *Even to date, people in this community call him deaf. So, sometimes you hear people shouting after him, hey, deaf! But that is not his name. He has his own name which his father gave him when he was born. Imagine that you give birth to a child and, because of [a] disease, or unexpected event, they abandon his name and call him deaf!*
>
> *Even her own brother's wife calls her nicknames. Can you imagine? So even in the house, when it is night, we close ourselves in our own little space and sleep and when day breaks, she goes on to the street and then we all go back to our work.*

The fact that society can substitute a person's name with his or her disability and abandon his or her name could be emotionally harrowing for the individual with disability, but more so for the family, particularly the parents. It is worth noting that in Ghanaian cultures, a name that is given to an individual has particular meaning for the family, and there are strong beliefs that names have implications for shaping the future and identity of their bearers (Abarry, 1991; Achemfuor, 2018). Therefore, parents and family members attach a certain sense of importance and connection to the names they give to their relatives. Hence, while the derogatory names that are often given to persons with disabilities (Baffoe, 2013, Moasun, 2023) inflict some level of emotional pain on family members, witnessing society abandon a name they give to their relative and label them with different and often derogatory ones can be very hurtful to families, as demonstrated in the excerpt above.

WITNESSING RELATIVES WITH DISABILITIES FACE CHALLENGES WITH FINDING MARRIAGE PARTNERS

In this chapter, we have already discussed the fact that families with relatives who have disabilities in Ghana are stigmatized, and their members face daunting tasks in finding marriage partners. Hence, it is a no-brainer that their relatives, because of whom they face such challenges, would be in a far more difficult position with respect to this topic. However, observing relatives with disabilities struggle to get marriage partners can represent emotionally difficult experiences for families. Family members and caregivers shared some stories of their relatives' experiences with implications for their own psychological and emotional well-being as follows:

> *You know, my sister is very beautiful, and she attracts a lot of men but whenever a man approaches her and realizes that she is deaf, they withdraw.*

While in the above quote, it was the case that potential suitors withdrew on their own will, in this next excerpt, it is the family of the suitor that blocked their son from marrying the woman because she had a disability:

> *My sister for instance, there was a time she wanted to marry. This guy was dating her for a while. But when it came to the time for them to regularize their relationship in the form of marriage, the parents of the guy said no, he shouldn't marry a disabled person [*sic*]. So, it actually touched my heart.*

This other quote suggests a general phenomenon in the participant's community, as her son is unable to find a wife due to his disability.

> *[H]e is the oldest of my children, he is very strong, stronger than any of his siblings, but he has no wife. The one following him is married and has two children. The next one too is married. But he is the one who is stronger and the oldest, but because of his hearing difficulty, he is not married because people say he is a deaf and deaf people are very difficult.*

In Ghanaian culture, marriage and childbearing are important in asserting the personhood and status of individuals in society (Elleamoh & Dake, 2019). Earlier in this chapter, we discussed the fact that persons with disabilities are already low in personhood due to their disabilities and inability to provide help as expected by society. Hence, their failure to get married and therefore reproduce children would only further lower their personhood and status in society, leading to deeper stigma and discrimination against them. While this directly impacts the lives of persons with disabilities, their relatives and caregivers who witness these experiences may themselves be adversely impacted psychologically and emotionally.

Disability, as you may already know, can occur at different stages of a person's life (Kittay, 2011). While some may be born with their conditions, others may acquire them later in life. So far, we have discussed the experiences of persons with disabilities with respect to the onset of disability prior to their attempts to get married. However, evidence from our research suggests that even if one experienced a disabling condition while being happily married, they were not spared disability-related stigma and discrimination, which negatively affected their marriages. When such an event happens and marriages break down, family members are affected in diverse ways. They may assume the responsibility of caring for their relatives, may directly experience disability-related stigma, and, as evident in the following quote, they may also be indirectly impacted as they share in the sorrows of their relatives with disabilities:

> *She had been returned from her husband's home three times. On previous occasions, her father had advised her not to return to her husband's place, but she would not listen. On the first two occasions [when she was returned], she got well. But the third time, the one [herbalist] who had twice treated her had died, so who would treat her this time?*

To give context to the above excerpt, the individual in question had a mental health condition. She had been married and lived with her husband until she started experiencing mental illness, and then her husband sent her packing to her parents' home. It is also important to note that the woman in question only experienced episodes of mental instability after delivering a child. This is suggestive of post-partum depression (Atuhaire et al., 2020). But without proper mental health care after multiple episodes, she had become chronically ill. It is worth reiterating that in Ghana and most parts of Sub-Saharan Africa, belief in supernatural causes of a disability is rife, such that it does not matter when and how the condition occurs but that any cause of disability must first be permitted spiritually before it happens in the physical realm (Devleiger, 2015).

It is also worth reminding that disabilities and impairments have often been attributed to the sins of individuals and their relatives (Agbenyega, 2003; Devlieger, 2015). Thus, a daughter returning from hermarital home because of a disability has implications for not only the way the husband's family perceives the wife and her family but also how other members of the family's community will perceive them. All these may constitute sources of stress for families whose relatives are returned from their marital homes because of the onset of a disability. In the next part of this chapter, we discuss the impact of disability stigma and discrimination on families and caregivers.

IMPACT OF DISABILITY STIGMA AND DISCRIMINATION ON FAMILY MEMBERS AND CAREGIVERS

In this chapter so far, we have discussed direct and indirect experiences of disability stigma and discrimination by relatives and caregivers of persons with disabilities. In this section, our aim is to discuss the impacts of these experiences on them. We note here with emphasis that, whether direct or indirect experiences of stigma and discrimination, the impact on victims is similar in magnitude and requires prompt attention to address them. In general, the impact of stigma and discrimination on any individual may include reduced hope and aspirations, lower self-esteem, and difficulties in relationships (American Psychiatric Association, n.d.). You will see as we present and discuss the impact of disability stigma and discrimination against family members and caregivers that they were affected emotionally, psychologically, and physically.

EMOTIONAL AND PSYCHOLOGICAL IMPACT

The emotional and psychological impacts of disability stigma and discrimination are perhaps among the most important ramifications of family members and caregivers' experiences of disability stigma and discrimination. To think of the fact that they have done nothing wrong, they themselves do not have disabilities (not to say that having a disability is a justifiable basis for stigma and discrimination), and that their only "crimes" are because they have relationships with persons with disabilities or simply because they provide care for a human being who is different can invoke deep emotional and psychological reactions.

Strong emotional and psychological reactions to a negative event have implications for the poor emotional and psychological well-being of a person (Silván-Ferrero et al., 2020; Trani et al., 2020). It is no wonder our research reveals deep emotional and psychological reactions and effects for family members and caregivers of persons with disabilities. These were profoundly expressed by participants of our research across Ghana, including feelings of pain, sorrow and sadness, frustration, and loneliness.

Feelings of Pain, Sorrow, and Sadness

Across the country, family members and caregivers of persons with disabilities expressed feeling pained, sorrowful, and sad when they are stigmatized and discriminated against or when they observe the same treatments toward their relatives with disabilities. The following excerpts demonstrate the extent to which disability-related stigma and discrimination emotionally affect family members and caregivers of persons with disabilities:

> *In fact, when she does that to her [calls her names], it is like pouring hot water or pepper into my flesh. That is how it pains me. That is how I feel about it. It is God who has been keeping me going. Otherwise, when she does that, I feel like fire burning my skin. If I know where God is, I will go and ask God what I have done to deserve this in my life. But I don't know where he is.*

When it happens like that, I feel sorrowful. I feel pity for her too. The children always feel sad and her siblings too. They are always showing concern for her.

The latter excerpt is a vivid description of the fact that disability-related stigma and discrimination impact the emotions of family members of all ages. Particularly where children are involved, there is the potential for them to experience some level of psychological trauma apart from the emotional pain that they go through. Some of these children could grow up lacking confidence, self-esteem, and assertiveness (An et al., 2020). As will be discussed shortly, there is a potential for family members, particularly the children, to withdraw from social interactions, which results in social isolation and loneliness (Silván-Ferrero et al., 2020).

The following excerpts confirm painful feelings for family members who either experience stigma and marginalization or witnesse their relatives with disability experiencing such mistreatments:

When they call me this way [Bruku's Mother], it hurts me because I have a name and I wish they would call me by my name and not by my son's condition. I don't like it at all.

Sometimes I cry. I do not feel good about it all. After all, no matter what she has become, she is still my mother. Without her, I will not be in this world. So, I must not be ashamed of her.

I feel very, very bad. When it happens like that and I go home, I am unable to sleep. I think a lot about it. . . . [I]t is because of blindness, people treat me like this.

It is important to reiterate that the emotional reactions shown in the foregoing excerpts are only symptoms of the internal trauma that family members go through when they experience disability-related stigma and discrimination. There are significant psychological and mental health implications when people are sleep-deprived (Almarzouki et al., 2022). In all the above cases, it is obvious the families and caregivers have had to live with these negative experiences for as long as they have had relatives with disabilities in their families. This, more than anything else, means that they have been experiencing such negative emotions for an extended period. Thus, they are more likely than not to experience significant physical and mental health effects of stigma and discrimination.

Isolation and Loneliness

We have already made the case earlier in this chapter of how stigma and discrimination manifested in social exclusions and friends distancing themselves from family members and caregivers of persons with disabilities. Such social exclusions have implications for plunging relatives and caregivers not only into isolation but also making them lonely (Barreto et al., 2022; Kerr & Stanley, 2020). In the following excerpts, family members and caregivers shared the effects of stigma and discrimination on their desires to socially interact with others in their communities:

> *Sometimes I will be expressing myself among my colleagues and someone will just shut me up that "look at that blind woman's daughter too." So sometimes I just try to keep to myself so that nobody insults me.*
>
> *You know for the children; they cannot handle it and so sometimes they don't want to play with other children because they fear that they will use their mother's blindness to insult them. So, I keep advising them to forget about what the others tell them and try and mingle with them. To try and be part of them.*
>
> *Sometimes I am not happy being a sister to him or even having him as a brother. Sometimes I just sit alone, think of it, and try to forget about it and keep my life going.*

While social isolation generally leads to feelings of loneliness, we see in the case of the latter excerpt that the participant did not only isolate herself, but she was also beginning to develop feelings of shame about having a brother with mental illness. Such a development does have ramifications for her own emotional and psychosocial well-being, but more importantly, for the care of her brother (Mfoafo-M'Carthy et al., 2020). The feelings of shame that come with being related to a person with disability were so aggravated that the participant in the excerpt below went beyond socially isolating himself to fleeing from the community altogether because he could no longer withstand the psychological impact of the stigma and discrimination meted out to him when he wanted to marry a woman with hearing and speech impairments. The participant shared his experience as follows:

> *[S]ometimes when they said bad things about it [relationship], I did not want to go out. I kept myself indoors for almost the whole day. Finally, their words got into me, and I was very sorry for myself. . . . Because of that, I even travelled to Akosombo [a town in a different region from his home region] for three months because of the way people were treating me because of her. But still when I came back the story was still the same.*

To the extent that the participant will leave his community in order to avoid being stigmatized as a result of his relationship with a person with disability speaks to the challenges involved when persons with disabilities seek to find love and marriage (Acheampong et al., 2018; Moasun, 2019). In the context of the topic of discussion, however, we find how negatively impactful such stigmatizing attitudes from society can be on the mental health and well-being of persons who fall in love with individuals with disabilities. It is apparent from the foregoing excerpt that without mental fortitude and determination, persons who fall in love with individuals with disabilities would not be able to push through with marriage and settlement with them.

Frustrations

An important psychological impact of stigma and discrimination against family members and caregivers of persons with disabilities is that many become frustrated and lose hope in their relatives with disabilities. A typical case was this young lady who could no longer bear the stigma and other challenges that came with having a brother with mental illness:

> *I am very disturbed. Just recently I even tried doing whatever I can to make sure he is out of this house, even this town. I wish I can get something to just do for him to leave the house and go elsewhere so that even if I go to meet him somewhere, (sobs) like I will know that he is my brother alright. It would have been better than him living in the house here. Because the longer he continues to live here, it gives them problems. For instance, they can't sleep at night, they can't eat and a whole lot. And my father and my mother are thinking of it every day. And me, I am always disturbed.*

A critical reading of the above excerpt suggests mixed emotions, almost to the extent of a state of confusion. On the one hand, the love and affinity the family has for their relative with mental illness means they cannot afford to lose him. On the other hand, their experiences of stigma and discrimination by members of their society put unbearable pressure on them, such that the family would get him out of the sight of their community so that they can maintain some serenity and peace of mind. The experience of this family gives context to why many families in sub-Saharan Africa tend to hide their relatives with disabilities from the sight of the public (Opoku et al., 2018). If they are unable to hide their relatives with disabilities, some families tend to give in to killing them altogether (Allotey & Reidpath, 2001; Attafuah, 2000; Cimpric, 2010; Denham et al., 2010; Kassah et al., 2012).

OVERBEARING CARE RESPONSIBILITIES

Stigma and discrimination against families who have relatives with disabilities are often accompanied by neglect and a lack of the support needed by families and caregivers to provide and care for their relatives. Leaving often intense care responsibilities to families that are mostly impoverished and in the hands of older adults, which is often the case in the context of Ghana, can be emotionally draining as well as physically unbearable. This can leave caregivers overburdened and burned out (Innstrand et al., 2002; Kim, 2017). In the quote below, the participant, who was in her 1980s and the primary caregiver of her daughter with mental illness (in her late 40s), shares her experience as follows:

I decided that I was not going to take her to any place again. I do not have the energy; I don't have the strength; I can't handle it anymore. Even if people tell me that there is a very good place where she can be healed, I do not have the strength to take her there.

In chapter 3, we shared how this particular participant could not find people to help her get her daughter who has a mental illness to board a bus due to disability stereotype. From the foregoing excerpt, we do infer not only burnout but also severe frustration and a loss of hope in her daughter's future. More concerning is the uncertainty around the source of care and support for the daughter once her old mother gets called up by her maker. This situation prevails in Ghana and other sub-Saharan African countries and incites further research to ascertain the implications for the mental and emotional health of caregivers who are advanced in age and worry about the well-being of their dependent relatives when the former would have died. In the following quote, the frail caregiver gives further detail of the impact of her care responsibilities on her psychological and physical health and her worries about the future:

It has aged me more quickly than I would have aged. I don't think I should have been this frail. But too much thinking has caused me to grow this old so quickly. . . . It is the grace of God that I am still alive and am able to take care of her in my own little way. If I should die and leave her, imagine what will become of her. How will she survive?

The concern of the participant about what becomes of her daughter when the former dies is legitimate, considering that streets and major towns in Ghana are dotted with individuals with mental illness who have been neglected and abandoned by their families, communities, and government at large (Opoku et al., 2017; Mfoafo-M'Carthy et al., 2020; Zuurmond et al., 2018).

In other instances, the neglect of families and caregivers of persons with disabilities due to stigma and discrimination has often resulted in some direct caregivers and their relatives entering the streets to beg in order to feed themselves, as evident in the two excerpts below:

Her older brother sometimes supports a little, but not enough. So, she has to go around begging before we can have something to feed. . . . Some people give her corn and then she will bring it and if the children return from school, I will use it to prepare food for them to eat.

I have experienced a lot of problems with my mother. Even with eating alone, unless I go with my mother to solicit for food, it is difficult for us to get food to eat. It is a big challenge for me.

From these quotes, we see that poverty can combine in specific ways with stigma and discrimination to negatively impact the ego and pride of family members and caregivers of persons with disabilities. For instance, begging in any community is associated with shame and pity (Kassah, 2008; Walker, 2014). Thus, it takes a lot of guts for family members and caregivers to choose to enter the streets to beg for food in order that they and their dependent relatives with disabilities might be fed. In the penultimate section of this chapter, we present and discuss strategies that families and caregivers have adopted to cope with disability stigma and discrimination.

MECHANISMS ADOPTED BY FAMILY MEMBERS AND CAREGIVERS TO COPE WITH DISABILITY STIGMA AND DISCRIMINATION

Despite their experiences of stigma and discrimination and the resulting impacts on their lives, family members and caregivers of persons with disabilities continue to render indispensable and sometimes lifesaving care to their relatives with disabilities. The resolute nature of the commitments of some caregivers warrants that we throw light on how they are able to live and care for persons with disabilities in sometimes extremely toxic environments. Hopefully, others can learn from them. Our interviews of family members and caregivers across Ghana revealed different mechanisms that were adopted to cope with their negative experiences. In this section, we present three mechanisms, including accepting their situations as a design of fate, leaving it all to God, and taking solace in the fact that others might be experiencing worse situations. It is worth noting that the coping mechanisms employed by family members and caregivers were similar to those employed by persons with disabilities. Thus, at the risk of sounding repetitive from those mechanisms employed by persons with disabilities as seen in chapter 4, we re-present and discuss similar mechanisms employed by family members and caregivers as a way of emphasizing these mechanisms for the benefit of the reader.

ACCEPTING THE SITUATION AS PART OF THEIR FATE

As demonstrated in the preceding chapters, Ghanaians, like all Africans, are highly spiritual and attribute a lot of the events that occur in their daily lives to ordinations of supernatural powers (Mbiti, 1969). As a result, it is not uncommon for Ghanaians to resign from finding solutions to negative events in their lives and attributing them to fate designs. Our research confirmed that, in the face of extreme disability stigma and discrimination and their dire consequences for families' well-being, most families did not do much to confront stigma and discrimination. Most tended to accept such mistreatments as having been designed by fate.

> *Truly, upon all of the stigma, and the challenges, we cannot leave this community. If we leave, where shall we go? It is going to be like this everywhere. So, we have to accept it the way it is and live here patiently. . . . It is not that I do not feel the pain. I do. But I also know that blindness is given by God, and I cannot question God. Because that is how God has said it should be. So, I just don't show how bad I feel about it.*
>
> *I cannot do anything about it. . . . I don't have anything I can do about it. It is only God who can do something about the way people treat those who are unfortunate to be plagued with such a bad situation.*

From the excerpts, it is apparent that by accepting their experiences as matters of fate, families and caregivers prepare themselves mentally and emotionally to receive whatever negative treatments are meted out to them. It is worth noting from the first quote that the pervasive nature of disability stigma and discrimination leaves families with no hope as they feel they are unable to change deep-seated behaviors in their communities and yet are not certain that relocating to other towns would be any different. While in the presenting circumstances, families give up hope and try to cope with disability-related stigma and discrimination, we have been made aware of the potential impact of stigma and discrimination on the emotional, psychological, and physical well-being of family members and caregivers of persons with disabilities (Almarzouki et al., 2022; An et al., 2020; Silván-Ferrero et al., 2020; Trani et al., 2020). Hence, this type of coping mechanism can only be a short-term survival measure. Government and other stakeholders ought to do a lot by way of policy and practice interventions to find lasting solutions to disability-related stigma and discrimination in Ghanaian societies.

LEAVING IT TO GOD

Similar to accepting their disability experiences as designed by faith, leaving things to God was another common theme in respect of how families coped with disability stigma and discrimination. Many participants believed that whatever was happening to them was with God's permission and therefore had the tendency to leave things to God to use His own course to provide solutions to their negative experiences. Some of them do so by committing their conditions to prayer and asking God to take control over their situation.

> *Nobody likes it that his son should be deaf. But when it comes unexpectedly, what will you do? There is nothing you can do. I don't like it, it hurts me, but what will I do? Whatever I do, my son will remain a deaf and they will still call me by his condition. So, all I do is to remain patient and pray to God.*

Even as many prayed to God for His intervention at His own time, others, as can be seen from the excerpts below, simply did nothing but left their fate to God.

> *What can I do? I only exercise patience and leave it to God. I feel like it is the gift that God has given to me. Everyone born into this world is given a gift by God and I feel that it is my gift from God, and I have to cope with it. She is a human being, and it was my choice to marry her, so I have to cope with all the challenges that come with it and live with her.*
>
> *I try to be quiet and to allow the will of God to take its course and to live peacefully with everybody. I cannot leave this town. I cannot also create my own village and go to live there and if I go to a different town at all, maybe it will be worse, so I have to remain patient and live here like that.*

Here again, it can be inferred from the excerpt that the participant envisaged similar mistreatments even if he and his family relocated to a different community. This reiterates the pervasiveness of stigma and discrimination against individuals with disabilities and their families in Ghanaian communities.

COMPARING THEIR SITUATION TO OTHERS THAT ARE WORST

A final coping mechanism adopted by many families and caregivers was to compare their situations with those of others they were aware of and take solace in the fact that they were not alone in that position. The fact that, by these comparisons, families found that their situations might have been better gave them reason to be thankful to God and to continue taking care of their relatives with disabilities:

> *There are other families with persons with disabilities but like I said, when you see it and you look at yourself, you also thank God for what he has done for you.*

In spite of the fact that these comparisons may be good ways to cope with disability stigma and discrimination, coping should be seen only as the first stage of dealing with stigma and discrimination rather than as the only way. It might be helpful for families with similar experiences to come together to confront society on their experiences. This means key stakeholders in the welfare industry must work to mobilize families and caregivers of persons with disabilities and the necessary resources to combat such negative attitudes and behaviors toward persons with disabilities and their families.

The United Nations Children's Fund [UNICEF] (n.d.) suggests that combating disability-related stigma and discrimination requires interventions that target multiple socio-ecological levels, multiple audiences, and combine communications, advocacy, and programming. A scan of literature (American Psychiatric Association, n.d.; Virendrakumar et al., 2021; UNDSPD & UNDESA, n.d.; UNICEF, n.d.) suggests several actions that can be undertaken to address disability-related stigma and discrimination. These include, among other actions:

- Empowering persons with disabilities and their families by helping them to develop leadership and advocacy skills, so as to help them overcome the shame that often accompanies disability.
- Encouraging persons with disabilities and their families to talk openly about disability in public spaces. This may also include facilitating contact between persons with disabilities and their families, and the community so that the community becomes more exposed to the realities of persons with disabilities and their families.
- Developing community-based sensitization and taking steps to educate persons with disabilities themselves and their relatives.
- Educating society to be conscious of the language they use to refer to persons with disabilities and their relatives.
- Encouraging the public to show compassion for persons with disabilities and their families rather than pity.

CONCLUSION

This chapter discussed disability-related stigma and discrimination as experienced by family members and caregivers of persons with disabilities in Ghana. We have come to understand that family members and caregivers of persons with disabilities may experience direct and indirect stigma and discrimination within their communities. We have learned through this chapter that whether stigma and discrimination were direct or indirect, the severity of their impacts on family members and caregivers of persons with disabilities is essentially the same.

The impact of disability stigma and discrimination as presented in this chapter includes various forms of emotional and psychological effects on victims, and physical effects such as unbearable care responsibilities that emerged because of neglect and a lack of support to families and caregivers. We have learned that such unbearable burdens result in burnout and the loss of hope for family members and caregivers. Despite the stigma and discrimination that families and caregivers face because of their relationships with persons with disabilities, and despite the negative consequences of these experiences, family members and caregivers continued to care for their relatives. They adopted different coping mechanisms, including unconditionally accepting the situation as part of their fates, leaving their grievances to God to intervene at His own time, and taking solace in the fact that others may be experiencing worse situations than they are. The chapter ends with a suggestion of different ways to deal with disability-related stigma and discrimination.

NOTE

1. "Bruku" is a Dagbani word that literally translates as "dumb."

Part III

THE WAY FORWARD

Chapter 6

Doing Disability Research in Ghana

Lessons Learned and Recommendations

INTRODUCTION

Doing research in Third World countries can be as daunting as it can be fulfilling. Research that is set in rural areas in developing countries can be difficult to conduct as communities are usually physically inaccessible due to poor road conditions. In addition, there could be challenges finding accommodation, food, and other essential commodities, as these may not be commercially available. While these may represent the downside of researching rural communities, in social science research projects involving human participants, populations may be easily accessible, reducing the stress that often accompanies the recruitment of participants in the developed world as well as in major cities of the developing world. In this chapter, we discuss our experiences researching disability in Ghana spanning into decades. We discuss experiences gathered from the research process, some key learning moments, and recommendations for research, policy, and practice with persons with disabilities.

UPS AND DOWNS OF DOING DISABILITY RESEARCH IN GHANA

As academics who have engaged in disability research in Ghana for decades, we have accumulated pleasant and unpleasant experiences that are worth sharing with the academic and non-academic communities in our bid to contribute to shaping disability research, policy, and practice. Particularly as researchers who are based outside of Ghana, our experiences are peculiar compared to researchers who are based in Ghana. As non-residents of Ghana, conducting research in rural communities in Ghana presents additional challenges involving struggles with securing accommodation, finding food, and other essential commodities to buy in rural communities where there are no hotels, guest houses, or food vendors, as all households prepare and serve food domestically.

In order to traverse these challenges, we have had to rely on local research assistants and contact persons, who are, in many instances, hard to come by. Over the years, in many cases, we have come to rely on the proverbial Ghanaian hospitality to meet our accommodation and feeding needs when we do research in rural communities. Individuals would vacate their rooms in order to accommodate us in some instances, even when they might be meeting the researcher for the first time. Women in rural communities are always willing to part with a bowl of food to make the "strange" researcher comfortable. In essence, while such facilities may not be readily available in rural communities, they may be highly affordable and may help to cut down on the fiscal cost of conducting research. It is important to caution researchers to be sure to compensate persons who sacrifice their homes and resources to accommodate and facilitate their stays in rural communities to do research. We have found it both stressful to do disability research in rural Ghana and fulfilling when we build lasting relationships with communities and research participants. The compensations that we have given to sometimes very impoverished individuals and their families for accommodating and feeding us have been found to go a long way toward cushioning them against the impact of poverty.

Besides the social aspect of researching in rural areas of Ghana, which can be challenging, we have found the actual research process to be smooth and less demanding. Research participants are readily available and willing to participate. Despite the tendency for some families to hide their relatives with disabilities from public sight (Bark et al., 2011; Bonsu & Yendork, 2019; Gyamfi & Hegadoren, 2017), and therefore, being referred to in research parlance as a hard-to-reach or hidden population, we have found it rather easy to recruit persons with disabilities and their families in rural communities.

Strategies, including appropriate community entry techniques, building rapport with key personalities within communities, and approaching potential participants with empathy and genuineness, have facilitated our recruitment processes (Appiah, 2020). The snowball sampling technique has proven helpful, but also participants who are impressed by their interactions with researchers have often spread the news of the presence of the researchers in communities, sometimes leading to an overwhelming number of people coming forward to be interviewed. In an instance in a community in the northern part of Ghana, a contact person had informed the disability community of the research and the research team recruiting persons with disabilities and their families or caregivers to be interviewed for the project that formed the basis of this book. By the time the research team arrived at a pre-arranged venue to meet the contact person, there was a gathering of more than fifty people with disabilities and their family members waiting to be interviewed. In situations like these, researchers must be careful not to abuse the research process. Patience and care must be taken to ensure informed consent and other research protocols are followed. Often, in rural communities, participants are not concerned about such protocols. Once they are convinced about the project, they are ready to be interviewed immediately. However, being cognizant of the negative implications of research with human participants and the additional vulnerabilities of persons with disabilities, researchers must ensure strict adherence to culturally appropriate research ethics.

An important lesson we learned from our recruitment of people with disabilities and their family members to participate in our research projects is that many of them were motivated by the compensation that came with their participation. In the following section, we discuss the intricate connection between poverty and disability. This situation means that the least amount of money that individuals and families can receive by participating in a research project is attractive enough for them to want to take part in the research. This also means that even if participants have concerns about the research, they might overlook these concerns in order to get the money that is sometimes enough to feed them and their families for a week. In this situation, the ethical requirement is that compensation to research participants must be such that it is adequate to make up for the time spent but not too much to coerce participants to take part in the study (Tri-Council of Canada, 2014). This presents a dilemma for doing research with impoverished individuals with disabilities and their families. In the sense of the true meaning of coercion as defined by the Tri-Council, even a penny given to an individual with disability and/or their family member who participates in a study would be appealing enough for them to want to participate in the study. To this effect, the onus lies with the researcher to conduct research with poor participants with genuine intention and purpose, in spite of the potential for individuals to participate in research because of the compensation amount, no matter how small the amount.

THE DISABILITY-POVERTY NEXUS

One of the most important lessons we learned from our study of disability in Ghana is that disability and poverty are intricately connected, such that dealing with the negative experiences of disability will mean addressing poverty among individuals with disabilities and their families. Extant literature suggests poverty to be both a cause and a consequence of disability (Metts,

2004; Mitra et al., 2011). Meekosha (2008) posits that in the Global South, including countries like Ghana, "disability and poverty go hand in hand" (p. 3). Jolley et al. (2017) suggest that this relationship between poverty and disability is particularly strong in sub-Saharan Africa. Nepveux (2009) cites Choruma (2006) to have characterized the connection between poverty and disability in Africa as "linked in a vicious circle, as people with disabilities are more prone to live in chronic poverty, which in turn can lead to disabling conditions" (Nepveux, 2009, p. 31).

Mitra et al. (2011), on their part, show that when disability occurs in a person's life, it may result in "lower living standard and poverty through adverse impact on education, employment, earnings, and increased expenditures related to disability" (Mitra et al., 2011, p. ii). Lord et al. (2010) corroborate that poverty may be responsible for the lack of investment, especially in children with disabilities. In Ghana, we found this to be particularly true as parents prefer to invest in the education of their children without disabilities to the neglect of those with disabilities (Boachie-Sarpong, 2012; Fiasorgbor & Ayagiyire, 2015; Reynolds, 2010; Voice Ghana, 2014). On the other hand, disability can be a source of poverty, as persons with disabilities are either unable to work or are refused employment due to stigma and discrimination (Geurts & Komabu-Pomeyie, 2016; Naami et al., 2012; Nepveux, 2009).

Again, some disability researchers have attempted to make the case that poverty can be a driving force in some of the negative beliefs about disabilities and the subsequent mistreatment of persons with disabilities in Ghana (Agbenyega, 2003; Denham et al., 2010; Fiasorgbor & Ayagiyire, 2015). Poverty, when combined with other factors such as ignorance and economic challenges, can accentuate accusations of children (with disabilities) as witches or evil in many parts of Africa (Cimpric, 2010; Jolley et al., 2017). Denham et al. (2010) found these assertions to be true for Ghana. While our research has not explored this topic in detail, our cumulative experiences garnered from many decades of researching disability in Ghana have given us the impression that persons with disabilities who were in relatively good economic and financial positions experienced better personhood, were treated relatively better, and enjoyed a good level of citizenship (Moasun, 2019).

Further to the foregoing discussion, our research on disability in Ghana has given us the impression that a significant part of the negative experiences of persons with disabilities and their families have risen out of neglect from society. While some elements of neglect of persons with disabilities and their families may be the result of fear arising out of spirituality and beliefs, as will be discussed shortly, we have significant reason to believe that a lot of the time, poverty engenders the neglect of the material needs of individuals with disabilities and their families. Literature affirms that in Ghana, the scarcity of resources coupled with extra needs for care by persons with disabilities may cause families to view persons with disabilities as liabilities and marginalize or neglect them (Boachie-Sarpong, 2012; Reynolds, 2010; Voice Ghana, 2014).

CULTURE AND BELIEF SYSTEMS AS THE BANE OF DISABILITY EXPERIENCES

Culture and belief systems and their relationships with disability and disability experiences for persons with disabilities and their families have been extensively discussed in this book. It should be apparent by now the extent to which culture and belief systems influence the (mis)treatments of persons with disabilities and their families. We have established in this book that what a society believes about a particular disability and its cause directs efforts at how people relate with individuals with disabilities. This assertion has been confirmed by several African disability literature (Boachie-Sarpong, 2012; Ingstad, 1990; Stone-McDonald & Butera, 2014). Therefore, if any country is to be able to effectively protect the rights of its citizens with disabilities, there must be conscious efforts to address negative beliefs about disability, persons with disabilities, and their families (Devlin & Pothier, 2006).

We have seen in this book that the maltreatments of persons with disabilities sometimes emanate from within the families of individuals with disabilities, even to the extent that some family members consent to and lead in the abandonment or murder of their relatives with disabilities. At the superficial level, many may be tempted to condemn individuals within the family who are complicit in the maltreatment of their relatives with disabilities. However, an important lesson we have learned about such involvements is that, besides the role of poverty, as discussed earlier, negative beliefs can cause fear and frustration in some family members who give in—against their will—to the maltreatment of their relatives with disabilities (Allotey & Reidpath, 2001; Bayat, 2015; Kiyaga & Moores, 2003; Slikker, 2009). Thus, as we attempt to protect persons with disabilities and their families, it is important for stakeholders to continue to avert their minds to the role of culture and belief systems in promoting and sustaining negative disability practices.

BELIEFS ABOUT MENTAL ILLNESS CONSTITUTE SEVERE BARRIERS TO INCLUSION

We have demonstrated in chapter 4 of this book that mental illness is one of the most stigmatized of the different forms of disability. The belief that mental illness is incurable, for example, puts persons who have been cured of mental illness in perpetual positions of stigma and discrimination. We find the proverb that "if a mentally ill person claims he has been cured, there remains a little to be used to intimidate children" to be pervasive in Ghanaian speeches. Such a posture means that once a person has been diagnosed with mental illness, society will always suspect them of retaining a certain level of mental instability, even if they are medically treated and discharged. This has implications for the reintegration of persons who are cured of mental illness. This means they would be unable to find jobs, for example, which in turn will condemn them to perpetual poverty.

On the other hand, we have established in this book that belief in spiritual causes of mental illness is pervasive in Ghana, leading to many families resorting to spiritual approaches to healing. While we do not contest the possibility of spiritual courses of mental illness, it is our considered opinion—informed by our many years of researching the topic—that many of the cases of mental illness that end up in religious places of worship would easily be treated if reported to hospitals in a timely manner. We are also aware that this problem is accentuated by the lack of mental healthcare institutions across the country. Worthy of note is also the fact that many prayer camps where persons with mental illness are taken for spiritual healing end up being dummy prisons which abuse and neglect individuals in their care, leading to aggravation of their conditions. The fact that these prayer camps are not under the regulation of any state agency, and that each camp operates under their own whims and caprices means persons under their care have no form of legal protection against abuse and neglect.

POLICY GAPS HAVE NEGATIVE IMPLICATIONS FOR PERSONS WITH DISABILITIES AND THEIR FAMILIES

It is our understanding that we do not necessarily lack policy and legal frameworks for the protection of persons with disabilities and their families. Article 29 of Ghana's national constitution makes provision for the protection of the rights of citizens with disabilities. In 2006, Ghana's parliament passed the Persons with Disability Bill into law (Act 715). Ghana's parliament also passed the Mental Health Bill into law (Act 846). In addition to these laws, Ghana's National Social Protection Policy (NSPP) generally provides a policy framework for the care of socially and economically vulnerable persons in the country, including those with disabilities. The Livelihood Empowerment Against Poverty is an offshoot policy of the NSPP. It hands out direct cash grants to beneficiaries to cushion them against the impact of extreme poverty (Ministry of Gender, Children, and Social Protection, 2015). The National Health Insurance Scheme (NHIS) is another social protection program run by the government of Ghana that provides important health benefits for persons with disabilities (National Health Insurance Authority, 2013).

Despite the existence of these policy frameworks to protect and guarantee the livelihood and well-being of persons with disabilities, we have seen from the chapter, how individuals with disabilities and their families continue to experience some extreme forms of stigma and discrimination. We do not speak to the abuse and neglect of persons with disabilities as they are not the subject of this book, but we do mention passively that these are as pervasive as stigma and discrimination. The continuous prevalence of maltreatment against persons with disabilities and their families and caregivers in spite of the existence of these legislative and policy frameworks suggests a need to interrogate the relationship between disability policy and practice. Such an interrogation, we believe, may begin with an analysis of the legislation and policy frameworks that give rise to the protection of persons with disabilities. As part of our research on disability in Ghana, we have done a rudimentary analysis of some of these disability policies and identified some lapses.

We identified poor targeting as one of the fundamental challenges for persons with disabilities to access the needed resources to enable their empowerment. In every policy, the definitions of the target population set the inclusion and exclusion criteria and must be done with some level of meticulousness. The National Health Insurance Policy provides free health insurance coverage for Ghanaian citizens who are extremely impoverished. This population has been referred to as "indigent." The National Health Insurance Regulation (LI 1809) proceeds to define an indigent as one who

> is unemployed and has no visible source of income; does not have a fixed place of residence according to standards determined by the scheme; does not live with a person who is employed and who has a fixed place of residence; and does not have any identifiable consistent support from another person. (p. 21)

Fundamentally, this definition is flawed on many fronts when it comes to persons with disabilities. For instance, to say that an indigent should be one who does not have a fixed place of residence is a failure to consider the realities of many persons living in destitution in Ghana. We make this argument on the basis that some of the individuals who shared their experiences of begging as shared in this book (see chapter 5) lived in what would be considered decent homes according to the standards of their communities. The realities of these individuals are that they cannot afford food to eat. Hence, if the government would not consider this reality but base a decision on whether they have a fixed place of residence, many of these would continue to be deprived of the necessary health benefits. This would mean additional financial responsibilities for their families as they are unable to subscribe to the health insurance policy, and when they fall ill, they would have to pay for healthcare services out of pocket. Effectively, this means, most persons with disabilities will not access formal healthcare as they simply are not in the position to pay for it.

Again, the criterion that an individual should not be living with a person who is employed is untenable for many persons with disabilities in Ghana, particularly those in rural areas. The Ghana Statistical Service (2013) considers anyone who is engaged in subsistence agriculture as being employed. However, most rural dwellers engaged in such economic activities are impoverished and can barely feed themselves during certain seasons of the year (Moasun, 2019). Thus, if a person with a disability lives with an impoverished subsistence farmer, they would not meet this criterion to be able to benefit from such a policy. The National Health Insurance Authority (NHIA), which is the implementing body of the NHIS, has been frustrated by this definition and expressed that it has hindered their ability to capture many of the very poor and vulnerable people (NHIA, 2013).

On the other hand, the Persons with Disability Act (Act 715), arguably the most important law for persons with disabilities besides the Constitution of the Republic, has been criticized for not capturing certain aspects of the lives of individuals with disabilities. The law, just like the constitution, has no provision on equality or non-discrimination on grounds of disability (Asante & Sasu, 2015). This leaves a vacuum that, in our understanding, may form a significant basis for some of the incidents of stigma and discrimination that have been discussed in this book. We have in this book acknowledged the peculiar role that cultural and philosophical understandings of disability play in the stigmatization and discrimination against persons with disabilities. We also acknowledge that culture and belief systems are difficult to change. However, we are convinced that adequate legal provisions can be the starting point for creating cultural shifts.

KINSHIP AS THE MAIN MOTIVATOR FOR THE CARE OF PERSONS WITH DISABILITIES

In chapter 5, we discussed family members and caregivers' experiences of stigma and discrimination simply because of their relationships with persons with disabilities. We saw in that chapter the impact of stigma and discrimination on families and caregivers. Yet, we also saw how resolute some family members and caregivers were in disposing of their care responsibilities toward their relatives with disabilities. One of the lessons we took away from the research is that blood relation or affinity was a strong motivator for individuals to continue to provide care for their relatives with disability despite the challenges. The following excerpts buttress this conclusion:

And where can we send her to? She has to stay with me. I am her mother. So, if her husband's people have rejected her and her children, I have to take them in and do the best that I can to take care of them.

With my father's disability, I would not say that I am happy, but this is a challenge that I have prepared myself to face. Because until he dies, there is nothing that anyone can do about the disability. People in the community know that my father has a disability, neighbors know that my father has a disability, my friends know that he has a disability, my wife knows that my father has a disability. But after everything, can I throw him away? I cannot throw him away. So, I feel it, but I live with him.

I cannot neglect my sister because she is my blood. She is my sister so if I see how she is suffering, the way people are discriminating against her, the way they are insulting her, myself and the children, I feel very bad about it . . .

The foregoing excerpts suggest that while family members and caregivers find their experiences of having and taking care of a relative with disability challenging, they are unable to give up because of their affinity with the latter. It is therefore important for stakeholders to consider how this motivator can be leveraged to ensure more enabling environments for persons with disabilities as well as their direct caregivers.

CONCLUSION

The prevailing stigma and discrimination against individuals and their family members and caregivers despite protective policy frameworks, albeit identified lapses above, means there is more to dealing with disability-related stigma and discrimination than legal and policy frameworks. We have established in this book that culture and belief systems are instrumental in the stigma and discrimination that individuals with disabilities and their families experience. This means to effect any positive change in regard to stigma and discrimination experienced by persons with disabilities and their families, efforts must target cultural and attitudinal changes. As we do so, we must bear in mind that change will be incremental and requires patience.

At the individual level, we must all commit to the following:

- Make critical effort to interact with and get to know at least a person with a disability. If possible, develop friendship with them. This way, we would understand disability and persons with disabilities better in order not only to avoid perpetuating harm against them but also to be advocates for positive change for persons with disabilities.
- In this book, we have shown how negative language can adversely impact persons with disabilities, their families, and caregivers. We invite you to

make conscious efforts to use appropriate and positive disability language both in your everyday communication and in your interactions with persons with disabilities.

- In Ghanaian and other developing country contexts, many persons with disabilities need help in order to survive and perhaps thrive. Considering this and as a result of limited government support for persons with disabilities, we implore you to help a person with disability whenever necessary. However, we beckon you to do so respectfully.
- Also in this book, we have made the case that negative attitudes constituted a significant source of the negative experiences of persons with disabilities in Ghana. We reckon that any change must begin at the individual level and invite you to engage in some introspection on your own thoughts and attitudes toward individuals with disabilities and to make efforts to correct any negative attitudes.
- Again, persons with disabilities are among the most vulnerable in society. Hence, they need every support that well-meaning members of society can offer them in order to ensure their protection and inclusion in society. As such, we invite you to be their ally and stand with them as they advocate for their rights.

Conclusion

Based on grassroots narratives, this book has explored the roots and impact of disability stigma in Ghana, focusing on persons with physical disabilities as well as those diagnosed with mental illness and their caregivers. Using qualitative methodologies, we sought to privilege the voices of our participants to reveal their daily experiences. Uniquely, we set up our analysis with an overview of the history of disability and stigma in Ghana, which is not usually done in studies of this type. The historical context is important for at least two reasons. First, it shows that stigma toward disability is deeply rooted in Ghanaian society and culture, but also that we can find examples of fair treatment and inclusion of persons with disabilities in African and Ghanaian history.

In the precolonial era, stigma was rooted in beliefs about the spiritual roots of disability, which are common in the oral traditions and epics that have been passed down and recorded over time. As presented in Chapter 2, thanks to the painstaking work of M. Miles, we know that communities in regions as diverse as Egypt, Ethiopia, Uganda, and Nigeria ascribe disability to spiritual forces. Appiah and Appiah's work on Ghanaian proverbs reveals similar beliefs in Ghanaian precolonial history. Second, the historical overview demonstrates that colonialism contributed to disability stigma by imposing Western notions of disability as a deviation from "normality," defined as the capacity for productive labor.

In the colonial era, the written record demonstrates the shift to a new type of disability stigma, in which personhood became attached to the capacity to perform productive work. Persons with disabilities were stigmatized as being inherently unproductive. This led to a charity model under which persons with disabilities were to be "normalized" through rehabilitation. Developed during the late colonial period, the rehabilitation model was taken up by independent Ghana's first leader, Kwame Nkrumah. During the 1960s, Ghanaians with disabilities would enjoy status as citizens only if they were rehabilitated sufficiently to join the "regular" labor market (Amuah, 1966). These aspects of precolonial and colonial Ghanaian history have contributed to disability stigma through cultural and spiritual beliefs that Ghanaians with disabilities are incapable on their own of being productive members of their communities, and that they can enjoy full citizenship only if they are rehabilitated and trained to be able to participate in productive economic activities.

Chapters 3 to 6 presented the inheritance and legacy of Ghanaian disability history through the testimonies of Ghanaians with disabilities about the experience and impact of stigma in their daily lives. Chapter 3 foregrounds culture as an important factor in disability stigma as manifested in language and indigenous beliefs about disabilities. Our discussion focused on Ghanaian language in the form of oral traditions, including epics, folk tales, stories, and folklore. Through these mediums, we argue that language operates as an important cultural tool for naming phenomena and defining cultural identities. In turn, identities include social and cultural norms that define relations between individuals in society, including insider and outsider status.

In Africa, many oral traditions ascribe negative labels to disability. From the literature, we found numerous instances of negative labeling of disability in Ghana, including currently used terms and disability language embedded in proverbs. These negative labels influence indigenous beliefs about disability, which are often connected to the spiritual realm. As such, indigenous Ghanaian beliefs not only feed into stigma but also lead people to look for spiritual solutions to reverse disabilities. As such, Ghanaians with disabilities are subjected to double stigmatization and marginalization: they are ostracized and shunned due to negative beliefs about disability, and they are denied material interventions that might help in favor of spiritual fixes that often make their situation worse. Underlying this marginalization are persistent stereotypes and myths about disability in Ghana. These include the assumption that persons with disabilities are incapable of productive work or that persons with mental illness or deafness are inherently aggressive or violent.

Related to stereotypes are myths about disability, such as the idea that women with disabilities will necessarily give birth to children with disabilities or the belief that families with children with disabilities are cursed. As with stereotypes, these kinds of myths lead to social isolation and misguided treatment and care for persons with disabilities. It is clear from our analysis that understanding stigma toward disability in Ghana requires an awareness of its foundation in culture and belief systems. One important implication of this chapter is that researchers and policymakers must pay attention to language in its cultural contexts in order to fully understand the stigmatization of Ghanaians with disabilities.

Chapter 4 narrows the cultural theme of the previous chapter by focusing on religion, spirituality, and mental illness in Ghana. The chapter argued that religion and spirituality play a very important role in mental health and mental illness in the Ghanaian context. Among Christians, Muslims, and communities practicing traditional religions, mental illness is often attributed to religious or supernatural causes, including possession by demons, witchcraft, or spiritual punishments for misdeeds or crimes. This fact has been well documented in the academic literature, and it is confirmed in the data from our fieldwork. Interestingly, many of our respondents themselves attributed their mental illnesses to spiritual causes. The internalization of this belief is an important finding in itself. But our data is unique as well, in that it shows clearly that religion can provide a refuge and coping mechanism for Ghanaians with disabilities in the face of stigma and discrimination. For our participants, these coping mechanisms included both individual beliefs and religious devotion, as well as institutionalized support from churches and mosques. In this sense, religion and spirituality fed into stigma but also provided a source of resilience. One implication of this finding, within the context of pervasive spirituality and Ghana, is the importance of involving religious and spiritual leaders in programs for mental health.

Chapter 5 moves from the spiritual to the material realm in surveying the impact of stigma on individuals with disabilities. The existing literature shows that stigma exists in multiple arenas, including the workplace, the community, the family, and even the healthcare sector. In the workplace, Ghanaians with disabilities are denied employment, mistreated at work, or fired if they acquire a disability. In communities and families, they are often shunned and harassed. In the healthcare sector, they are discriminated against and denied treatment. Our fieldwork confirms the existence of stigma in these arenas as well as its connection to the cultural and religious beliefs presented in the previous two chapters. Our respondents conveyed an inherent sense of stigmatization, in many cases feeling that they are treated as less important or even less human by their counterparts without disabilities. Not only does this affect them psychologically, but it also leads to marginalization and discrimination on many levels. The narratives that we collected revealed that Ghanaians with disabilities are routinely discriminated against in the workplace, denied the right to marry and physically abused. As a result, beyond social and economic marginalization, they experience harmful psychosocial effects that severely undermine their well-being.

There is an urgent need for collective efforts on the part of the Ghanaian government, NGOs, and other civil society organizations to combat stigma as a first step toward improving the lives and livelihoods of Ghanaians with disabilities.

Chapter 6 continues with the theme of the impact of stigma, but it shifts the focus to the families of Ghanaians with disabilities, a unique perspective not usually found in the literature. The discussion began with an overview of evidence for stigma and discrimination from families' perspectives, then proceeded to analyze its impact and coping mechanisms to help their loved ones develop strategies for resilience in the face of persistent stigmatization. The narratives collected from families across Ghana reinforce the reality of disability stigma in several areas, including (to name a few) social exclusion and the loss of friendships, negative labeling and name-calling, and barriers to dating and marriage. However, families and caregivers are affected as well, witnessing disrespect and stigma directed at their loved ones. This places significant stress on family members and caregivers. They experience emotional and psychological distress, feelings of pain and sadness, social exclusion due to discrimination by community members, and significantly increased burdens of caring for relatives with disabilities. In the face of these challenges, families and caregivers turn to coping mechanisms, including resigning themselves to their fate, leaving their predicaments in the hands of God, and comparing their situations to others who might be worse off. Taken as a whole, the themes investigated in this chapter point to the importance of involving families and caregivers of persons with disabilities in programs to combat disability stigma and discrimination, and to include resources for the families and caregivers themselves.

References

Abarry, A. S. (1991). The significance of names in Ghanaian drama. *Journal of Black Studies*, *22*(2), 157–167. Available at: https://www.jstor.org/stable/2784591

Abdullah, T., & Brown, T. (2011). Mental illness stigma and ethnocultural beliefs, values, and norms: An integrative review. *Child Psychology Review*, *31*, 934–948.

Abdulmalik, J., Olayiwola, S., Docrat, S., Lund, C., Chisholm, D., & Gureje, O. (2019). Sustainable financing mechanisms for strengthening mental health systems in Nigeria. *International Journal of Mental Health Systems*, *13*(1), 1–15.

Acheampong, E., Edusei, K. A., Anoma, J. E., Nakoja, C., & Afful, B. F. (2018). Expectations of and challenges in marriage among people with disabilities in the Yendi Municipality of Ghana. *Developing Country Studies, 8*(9). Available at: https://www.iiste.org/Journals/index.php/DCS/article/view/44133

Acheampong, E., Nadutey, A., Anokye, R., Agyei-Baffour, P., & Edusei, A. K. (2021). The perception of healthcare workers of people with disabilities presenting for care at peri urban health facilities in Ghana. *Health & Social Care in the Community*, 1–9. Available at: https://doi.org/10.1111/hsc.13496

Achebe, C. (1958). *Things fall apart.* London: William Heinemann Ltd.

Adewuya, A. O., & Makanjuola, R. O. A. (2005). Social distance towards people with mental illness amongst Nigerian university students. *Social Psychiatry and Psychiatric Epidemiology*, *40*(11), 865–868. https://doi.org/10.1007/s00127-005-0965-3

Adjei, P., Akpalu, A., Laryea, R., Nkromah, K., Sottie, C., Ohene, S., & Osei, A. (2013). Beliefs on epilepsy in Northern Ghana. *Epilepsy & Behavior, 29*, 316–321.

Adoo, J. S. (1963). Planning of rehabilitation. *Advance*, *38*(April), 13–17.

Adoo, J. S. (1964). The rehabilitation services in Ghana. *Advance*, *41*(January), 25–30.

Adu, P., Jurcik, T., & Grigoryev, D. (2021). Mental Health Literacy in Ghana: Implications for religiosity, education and stigmatization. *Transcultural Psychiatry*. Available at: https://doi.org/10.1177%2F13634615211022177

African Studies Centre, Leiden. (2023). Disability in Africa. Available at: https://www.ascleiden.nl/content/webdossiers/disability-africa

Agbenyega, J. S. (2002). *The need for transitional services for students with intellectual disabilities in Ghana.* Unpublished honours thesis, Faculty of Education. Clayton, Monash University.

Agbenyega, J. S. (2003). *The power of labelling discourse in the construction of disability in Ghana: Educational research, risks and dilemmas.* Paper Presented at the Australian Association for Research in Education. Available at: www.are.org.nz/are_info.html (Accessed October 20, 2011).

Ahmedani, B. K. (2011). Mental health stigma: Society, individuals, and the profession. *Journal of Social Work Values and Ethics, 8*(2), 414–416. https://www.ncbi.nlm.nih.gov/pmc/articles/PMC3248273/pdf/nihms342711.pdf

Alemu, A. (2007). Oral narratives as ideological weapon for subordinating women: The case of Jimma Oromo. *Journal of African Cultural Studies, 19*(1), 55–79.

Alhassan, A. K., & Ridwan, A. (2022). Historical portrayal of children with disabilities andexclusionary practices in Northern Ghana. *Human Arenas*, 1–29. Available at: https://doi.org/10.1007/s42087-02100265-4

Allotey, P., & Reidpath, D. (2001). Establishing the causes of childhood mortality in Ghana: The "spirit child." *Social Science and Medicine*, *52*, 1007–1012.

Almarzouki, A. F., Mandili, R. L., Salloom, J., Kamal, L. K., Alharthi, O., Alharthi, S., Khayyat, N., & Baglagel, A. M. (2022). The impact of sleep and mental health on working memory and academic performance: A longitudinal study. *Brain Science, 12,* 1525. Available at: https://doi.org/10.3390/brainsci12111525

Alvares, C. (2011). A critique of eurocentric social science and the question of alternatives. *Economic and Political Weekly*, *46*(22), 72–81. https://www.jstor.org/stable/23018594

Amedome, S. N., & Bedi, I. K. (2018). The effects of religion and locus of control on perception of mental illness. *Journal of Religion and Health*, *58*(2), 653–665. Available at: https://doi.org/10.1007/s10943-0180658-3

American Psychiatric Association (n.d). Stigma, prejudice and discrimination against people with mental illness. Available at: https://www.psychiatry.org/patients-families/stigma-and-discrimination

Amoako, J. B. (1975). *Division of rehabilitation status report.* Accra: Ghana Ministry of Labor, Social Welfare and Community Development.

Amosun, S. L., Nyante, G. G., & Wiredu, E. K. (2013). Perceived and experienced restrictions in participation and autonomy among adult survivors of stroke in Ghana. *African Health Sciences, 13*(1), 24–31.

An, E. M., Lee, S. J., & Chung, I. J. (2020). The effects of the stigma trajectory of adolescents in out-of-home care on self-esteem and antisocial behavior. *Children and Youth Services Review.* Available at: https://doi.org/10.1016/j.childyouth.2020.105167

Anbaran, F. F. (2016). "A whole way of life": Ontology of culture from Raymond Williams's perspective. *International Letters of Social and Humanistic Sciences*, *67*, 46–56. Available at: https://doi.org/10.18052/www.scipress.com/ILSHS.67.46

Anderson, Julie (2011). *War, disability and rehabilitation in Britain: "Soul of a Nation."* Manchester: Manchester University Press.

Angermeyer, M. C., Matschinger, H., Carta, M. G., & Schomerus, G. (2014). Changes in the perception of mental illness stigma in Germany over the last two decades. *European Psychiatry, 29*, 390–395. Available at: https://doi.org/10.1016/j.eurpsy.2013.10.004

Anthony, J. H. (2009). Access to education for students with autism in Ghana: Implications for EFA. *Paper Commissioned for the EFA Global Monitoring Report 2010, Reaching the Marginalized, UNESCO.* Available at: http://unesdoc.unesco.org/images/0018/001865/186588e.pdf

Appiah, P., Appiah, K. A., & Agyemang-Duah, I. (2007). *Bu Me Bɛ: Proverbs of the Akans*. Oxfordshire: Ayebia Clarke Publishing Limited.

Appiah, R. (2020). Community-based participatory research in rural African contexts: Ethico-cultural considerations and lessons from Ghana. *Public Health Reviews, 41*(1), 27. Available at: https://doi.org/10.1186/s40985-020-00145-2

Archer, T. (1931). *The proverb*. Cambridge, MA: Harvard University Press.

Arko-Achemfuor, K. (2018). Naming of children and meaning of names among the Akan of Ghana: Defining identities? *Southern African Journal for Folklore Studies, 28*(1). Available at: https://doi.org/10.25159/1016-8427/4294

Asamoah, M. K., Osafo, J., & Agyapong, I. (2014). The role of Pentecostal clergy in mental health-care delivery in Ghana. *Mental Health, Religion & Culture, 17*(6), 601–614. Available at: https://doi:10.1080/13674676.2013.871628

Asante, L. A., & Sasu, A. (2015). The Persons with Disability Act, 2006 (Act 715) of the republic of Ghana: The law, omissions and recommendations. *Journal of Law, Policy and Globalization, 36*, 62–68.

Attafuah, K. G. (2000). Enhancing disability rights in Africa: The Ghanaian experience. *Social Policy Studies, 1*(2), 34–44.

Atuhaire, C., Brennaman, L., Cumber, S. N., Rukundo, G. Z., & Nambozi, G. (2020). The magnitude of postpartum depression among mothers in Africa: A literature review. *Pan African Medical Journal, 25*(37). Available at: https://doi.org/10.11604/pamj.2020.37.89.23572

Avoke, M. (2001). Some historical perspectives in the development of special education in Ghana. *European Journal of Special Needs Education, 16*(1), 29–40.

Avoke, M. (2002a). Models of disability in the labelling and attitudinal discourse in Ghana. *Disability & Society, 17*(7), 769–777.

Avoke, M. (2002b). Some historical perspectives in the development of special education in Ghana. *European Journal of Special Needs, 16*, 29–40.

Baffoe, M. (2013). Stigma, discrimination and marginalization: Gateways to oppression of persons with disabilities in Ghana, West Africa. *Journal of Educational and Social Research, 3*(1), 187–198.

Baker, C., & Imafidon, E. (2020). Traditional beliefs inform attitudes to disability in Africa. Why it matters. *The Conversation*. Available at: https://theconversation.com/traditional-beliefs-inform-attitudes-to-disability-in-africa-why-it-matters-138558

Barasch, M. (2001). *Blindness: The history of a mental image in Western thought*. New York and London: Routledge.

Barke, A., Nyarko, S., & Klecha, D. (2011). The stigma of mental illness in Southern Ghana: attitudes of the urban population and patients' views. *Social Psychiatry and Psychiatric Epidemiology, 46*(11), 1191–1202.

Barreto, M., van Breen, J., Victor, C., Hammond, C., Eccles, A., Richins, M. T., & Qualter, P. (2022). Exploring the nature and variation of the stigma associated with loneliness. *Journal of Social and Personal Relationships*, *39*(9), 2658–2679. Available at: https://doi.org/10.1177/02654075221087190

Barton, L., & Oliver, M., Eds. (1997). *Disability studies: Past present and future.* Leeds: The Disability Press.

Baum, F., MacDougall, C., & Smith, D. (2006). Participatory action research. *Journal of Epidemiology and Community Health*, *60*(10), 854–857.

Bayat, M. (2015). The stories of "snake children": Killing and abuse of children with developmental disabilities in West Africa. *Journal of Intellectual Disability Research, 59*(1), 1–10. Available at: https:/doi.org/10.1111/jir.12118

Birukou, A., Blanzieri, E., Giorgini, P., & Giunchiglia, F. (2013). A formal definition of culture. In K. Sycara, M. Gelfand, & A. Abbe (Eds.), *Models for intercultural collaboration and negotiation. Advances in group decision and negotiation* (vol. 6). Dordrecht: Springer. Available at: https://doi.org/10.1007/978-94-007-5574-1_1

Blake, J. W. (1942). William Towerson's first voyage to Guinea, 1555-6. In *Europeans in West Africa* (pp. 360–392). London: Hakluyt Society.

Boachie-Sarpong, K. (2012). *Who is disabled in Ghana? Part 2*. Available at: https://www.ghanaweb.com/GhanaHomePage/NewsArchive/Who-Is-Disabled-In-Ghana-Part-2-240180

Bolle, K. W., Smith, J. Z., & Buxton, R. G. A. (2022). "M*yth.*" *Encyclopedia Britannica*. Available at: https://www.britannica.com/topic/myth

Bonsu, A. S., & Yendork, J. S. (2019). Community-based mental health care: Stigma and coping strategies among professionals and family caregivers in the eastern region of Ghana. *Issues in Mental Health Nursing*, 444–451. Available at: https://doi.org/10.1080/01612840.2018.1564158

Borsay, A. (2006). Disciplining disabled bodies: The development of orthopaedic medicine in Britain, c.1800–1939. In D. M. Turner & K. Stagg (Eds.), *Social histories of disability and deformity* (pp. 97–116). London: Routledge.

Botts, B. H., & Evans, W. H. (2010). Ghana: Disability and spirituality. *Journal of International of Special Needs Education, 13*, 32–39.

Bourdieu, P. (1990). *The logic of practice*. Cambridge: Polity Press.

Branson, J., & Miller, D. (2002). *Damned for their difference: The cultural construction of deaf people as disabled.* Washington, DC: Gallaudet University Press.

Braun, V., & Clarke, V. (2006). Using thematic analysis in psychology. *Qualitative Research in Psychology*, *3*, 77–101.

Brohan, E., Gauci, D., Sartorius, N., & Thornicroft, G. (2011). Self-stigma, empowerment and perceived discrimination among people with bipolar disorder or depression in 13 European countries: The GAMIAN-Europe study. *Journal of Affective Disorders, 129*, 56–63. Available at: https://doi.org/10.1016/j.jad.2010.09.001

Brydges, C., & Mkandawire, P. (2018). Perceptions and experiences of inclusive education among parents of children with disabilities in Lagos, Nigeria. *International Journal of Inclusive Education, 24*, 1–15.

Brydon, L., & Legge, K. (1996). *Adjusting society: The World Bank, the IMF, and Ghana*. London: Tauris Academic Studies.

Buchanan, Robert M. (2002). *Illusions of equality: Deaf Americans in school and factory*. Washington, DC: Gallaudet University Press.

Bunzel, D. (2007). Rehabilitation through work? Disability and the productivist road to participation in the East of Germany. *Journal of Historical Sociology, 20*(3), 362–383.

Burch, S. (2002). *Signs of resistance: American deaf cultural history, 1900 to World War Two*. New York: New York University Press.

Burress, J. R. (1980). *Developments in services for handicapped people: Africa: A project report*. Washington, DC: People-to-People Committee for the Handicapped.

Canadian Institutes of Health Research, Natural Sciences and Engineering Research Council of Canada, and the Social Sciences and Humanities Research Council of Canada [Tri-Council] (2014). Tri-council policy statement: Ethical conduct for research involving humans (TCPS2). Available at: http://www.pre.ethics.gc.ca/pdf/eng/tcps2-2014/TCPS_2_FINAL_Web.pdf

Charlton, J. I. (2000). *Nothing about us without us: Disability oppression and empowerment*. Berkeley: University of California Press.

Cimpric, A. (2010). *Children accused of witchcraft: An anthropological study of contemporary practices in Africa*. Dakar: UNICEF WCARO.

Cohen, D. (2001). *The war come home: Disabled veterans in Britain and Germany, 1914–1939*. Berkeley: University of California Press.

Corrigan, P. W., Morris, S. B., Michaels, P.J, Rafacz, J. D & Rusch, N. (2012). Challenging the public stigma of mental illness: A meta-analysis of outcome studies. *Psychiatric Services, 63*(10), 963–973. http://dx.doi.org/10.1176/appi.ps.201100529

Corrigan, P., & A. Watson (2002). Understanding the impact of stigma on people with mental illness. *World Psychiatry, 1*(1), 16–20.

Corrigan, P. W., Watson, A. C., Warpinski, A. C., & Gracia, G. (2004). Stigmatizing attitudesabout mental illness and allocation of resources to mental health services. *Community Mental Health Journal, 40*(4), 297–307.

Crabtree, D. (2013). *Models of disability: English agenda*. British Council. Available at: https://englishagenda.britishcouncil.org/sites/ec/files/Models%20of%20disability.pdf

Creswell, J., Ed. (2013). *Qualitative inquiry and research design: Choosing among five approaches* (3rd ed.). Thousand Oaks: SAGE.

Dake, F. A. A. (2019). "Cementing" marriages through childbearing in subsequent unions: Insights into fertility differentials among first-time married and remarried women in Ghana. *PLOS One*. Available at: https://doi.org/10.1371/journal.pone.0222994

Dako-Gyeke, M., & Asumang, E. S. (2013). Stigmatization and discrimination experiences of persons with mental illness: Insights from a qualitative study in Southern Ghana. *Social Work and Society International Online Journal, 11*, 5–8.

Dako-Gyeke, M., & Donkor, M. D. (2018). Experiences and perspectives of stigmatization and discrimination against people with epilepsy in Accra, Ghana. *Epilepsy & Behaviour, 87*(1), 101–107. Available at: https://doi.org/10.1016/j.yebeh.2018.07.025

Darko, K. (2017). List of all the monarchs of the Ashanti Kingdom till date. *OMG Voice*, May 16. Available at: https://omgvoice.com/lifestyle/ashanti-kings-kingdom/

Degnan, A., Berry, K., Humphrey, C., & Bucci, S. (2021). The relationship between stigma and subjective quality of life in psychosis: A systematic review and meta-analysis. *Clinical Psychology Review, 85*, 102003. Available at: https://doi.org/10.1016/j.cpr.2021.102003

Deku, P., & Vanderpuye, I. (2017). Perspectives of teachers regarding inclusive education in Ghana. *International Journal of Whole Schooling, 13*(3), 39–54.

Denham, A. R. (2017). *Spirit children: Illness, poverty, and infanticide in Northern Ghana*. Madison: The University of Wisconsin Press.

Denham, A. R., Adongo, P. B., Freydberg, N., & Hodgson, A. (2010). Chasing spirits: Clarifying the spirit child phenomenon and infanticide in Northern Ghana. *Social Science & Medicine, 71*, 608–615.

Dennett, D. (1976). Conditions of personhood. In R. Rorty (Ed.), *The identities of persons* (pp. 175–196). Berkeley: University of California Press.

Despouy, L. (1993). *Human rights and disabled persons.* United Nations Enable. Available at: http://www.un.org/esa/socdev/enable/dispaperdes0.htm

Devlieger, P. J. (2015). At the interstices of classification: Notes on the category of disability in Sub-Saharan Africa. In Disability as a fluid state. *Emerald Insight*, 69–101. Available at: https://doi.org/10.1108/S1479-3547(2010)0000005006

Devlin, R., & Pothier, D. (2006). Introduction: Toward a critical theory of dis-citizenship. In R. Devlin & D. Pothier (Eds.), *Critical disability theory: Essays in philosophy, politics, policy and law* (pp. 1–24). Vancouver: UBC Press.

Di Stafano, E. (2015). Disability and Latin American cultural studies: A critique of corporeal difference, identity and social exclusion. *Canadian Journal of Disability Studies, 4*(2), 49–76.

Dosu, B., & Maura Hanrahan, M. (2021). Barriers to drinking water security in rural Ghana: The vulnerability of people with disabilities. *Water Alternatives, 14*(2), 453–468.

Driedger, D. (1989). *The last civil rights movement: Disabled people's international.* London: Hurst & Co Publishers.

Dudley, J. R. (2000). Confronting stigma within the services system. *Social Work, 45*(1), 449–455. doi: 10.1093/sw/45.5.449

Dugbartey, A. T., & Barimah, K. B. (2013). Traditional beliefs and knowledge base about epilepsy among university students in Ghana. *Ethnicity & Disease, 23*, 1–5.

Dzorgbo, D.-B., & Gyan, S. (2016). Exploratory study of the current status of the rights and welfare of Ghanaian women: Taking stock and mapping gaps for new actions. *African Journal of Re-productive Health, 20*(3), 136–148.

Economic Commission for Africa (1980). *Situation of disabled persons in Africa*. Document prepared by the Economic Commission for Africa Regional Secretariat for the Regional Technical Meeting and Seminar, October 1–7 (Addis Ababa, Ethiopia), par.4[b], [e]. Available at: https://repository.uneca.org/handle/10855/7736

Economic Commission for Africa (1987). *Implementation of the world programme of action concerning disabled persons in African countries*. Document prepared by the Economic Commission for Africa Regional Secretariat for the Fifth Conference of African Ministers of Social Affairs, March 16–28. Yamoussoukro, Cote d'Ivoire.

Edara, I. (2017). Religion: A subset of culture and an expression of spirituality. *Advances in Anthropology, 7,* 273–288. Available at: https://doi.org/10.4236/aa.2017.74015

Edwards, J. (2014). Ghana's mental health patients confined to prayer camps. *The Lancet, 383*(9911), 15–16. Available at: https://doi.org/10.1016/S0140-6736(13)62717-8

Elleamoh, G. E., & Egbe, C. O. (2015). Experiences and effects of psychiatric stigma: Monologues of the stigmatizers and the stigmatized in an African setting. *International Journal of Qualitative Studies on Health and Well-Being, 10*(2015), 6–7.

Eskay M., Onu, V. C., Igbo, J. N., Obiyo, N., & Ugwuanyi, L. (2012). Disability within the African culture. *US-China Education Review B, 4*, 473–484.

Evnine, S. J. (2008). *Epistemic dimensions of personhood.* New York: Oxford University Press.

Ferguson, R. J. (2001). *We know who we are: A history of the blind in challenging educational and socially constructed policies.* San Francisco: Caddo Gap Press.

Fiasorgbor A. D., & Ayagiyire, T. (2015). Perception of rural people about persons with physical disability: The case of Yorogo-Yipala community. *American Journal of Health Research, 3*(3), 177–182.

Foucault, M. (1982). The subject and power. *Critical Inquiry, 8*(4), 777–795.

Ganle, J. K., Otupiri, E., Obeng, B., Edusie, A. K., Ankomah, A., & Adanu, R. (2016). Challenges women with disability face in accessing and using maternal healthcare services in Ghana: A qualitative study. *PLOS One, 11*(6), 1–13.

Gary, F. A. (2005). Stigma: Barrier to mental health care among ethnic minorities. *Issues in Mental Health Nursing, 26*, 979–999. Available at: https://doi.org/10.1080/01612840500280638

Gebrekidan, F. N. (2012). Disability rights activism in Kenya, 1959-1964: History from below. *African Studies Review*, *55*(3), 103–122.

Gerber, D. A. (2012). *Disabled veterans in history.* Ann Arbor: University of Michigan Press.

Geurts, K. L. (2015). On the worlding of Accra's rehabilitation training centre. *Somatosphere*. Available at: http://somatosphere.net/2015/04/on-the-worlding-of-accras-rehabilitation-training-centre.html

Geurts, K. L., & Komabu-Pomeyie, S. G. M. A. (2016). From "sensing disability" to seselelame: Non-dualistic activist orientations in twenty-first-century Accra. In S. Grech & K. Soldatic (Eds.), *Disability in the Global South: The critical handbook* (pp. 85–98). Switzerland: Springer International Publishing.

Ghana Statistical Service. (2013). *National analytical report: 2010 population and housing census.* Accra: GSS.

Goffman, E. (1963). *Stigma: Notes on the management of spoiled identity*. New York: Simon & Schuster.

Gooding, P. M. (2014). Change and continuity in mental health law: The long road to the United Nations convention on the rights of persons with disabilities and its implications for mental health and the law today. *European Journal of Current Legal Issues, 20*(3). Available at: http://webjcli.org/article/view/367/470

Goreczny, A. J., Bender, E. E., Caruso, G., & Feinstein, C. S. (2011). Attitudes toward individuals with disabilities: Results of a recent survey and implications of those results. *Research in Developmental Disabilities, 32*, 1596–1609.

Government of Ghana (1961). *Annual Report of the Department of Social Welfare and Community Development, 1960*. Accra: Government Printer.

Government of Ghana (1963). *Annual Report of the Department of Social Welfare and Community Development, 1962*. Accra: Government Printer.

Government of Ghana (1964). *Annual Report of the Department of Social Welfare and Community Development, 1963*. Accra: Government Printer.

Green, S. E. (2003). "What do you mean what's wrong with her?": Stigma and the lives of families of children with disabilities. *Social Science & Medicine, 57*(8), 1361–1374. Available at: https://doi.org/10.1016/s0277-9536(02)00511-7

Grischow, J. (2011a). Disability and rehabilitation in Late Colonial Ghana. *Review of Disability Studies*, *7*(3&4), 52–51.

Grischow, J. (2011b). Kwame Nkrumah, disability and rehabilitation in Ghana, 1957–66. *Journal of African History, 52*(2), 179–199.

Grischow, J. (2015). "I nearly lost my work": Chance encounters, legal empowerment and the struggle for disability rights in Ghana. *Disability & Society, 30*(1), 101–113.

Grischow, J., & Mfoafo-M'Carthy, M. (2022). *Disability rights and inclusiveness in Africa: The convention on the rights of persons with disabilities, challenges and change.* London: James Currey.

Guernsey, Nicoli, M., & Ninio, A. (2017). *Convention on the rights of persons with disabilities: Its implementation and relevance for the World Bank.* World Bank: Social Protection Unit, SP Discussion Paper No. 0712, June 2017. Available at: http://siteresources.worldbank.org/SOCIALPROTECTION/Resources/SP-Discussion-papers/Disability-DP/0712.pdf/

Guffey, M. E., Lowey, D., Rhodes, K., & Rogin, P. (2013). *Business communication: Process & product* (4th brief Canadian ed.). Nelson Education.

Gyamfi, N., Mprah Kwadwo, W., Mensah, I., Kwabena, B. C., & Mensah, P. A. (2022). "For me I see MINE to be a family sickness"–Consumers understand and perception of the etiology of mental illness in community-based residential facilities in Ghana. *Mental Health, Religion & Culture, 25*(1), 68–84. Available at: https://doi.org/10.1080/13674676.2021.2014431

Gyamfi, S., Hegadoren, K., & Park, T. (2018). Individual factors that influence experiences and perceptions of stigma and discrimination towards people with mental illness in Ghana. *International Journal of Mental Health Nursing, 27*(1), 368–377.

Haihambo, C., & Lightfoot, E. (2010). Cultural beliefs regarding people with disabilities in Namibia: Implications for the inclusion of people with disabilities. *International Journal of Special Education, 25*(3), 76–87. Available at: https://files.eric.ed.gov/fulltext/EJ909038.pdf

Hanlon, C., & Alem, A. (2020). A leap of faith for more effective mental health care. *The Lancet, 396*(10251), 584–585. Available at: https://doi.org/10.1016/S0140-6736(20)31295-2

Herrmann, L. K., Welter, E., Leverenz, J., Lerner, A. J., Udelson, N., Kanetsky, C., & Sajatovic, M. (2018). A systematic review of dementia-related stigma research: can we move the stigma dial? *The American Journal of Geriatric Psychiatry*, *26*(3), 316–331. Available at: https://doi.org/10.1016/j.jagp.2017.09.006

Holder, S. M., Peterson, E. R., Stephens, R., & Crandall, L. A. (2019). Stigma in mental health at the macro and micro levels. Implication for mental health consumers and professionals. *Community Mental Health Journal, 55*(3) 369–374. http://dx.doi.org/10.1007/s10597018-0308-y

Hosking, D. L. (2008). *Critical disability theory*. A paper presented at the 4th Biennial Disability Studies Conference at Lancaster University, UK, September 2–4.

Howell, C., Chalklen, S., & Alberts, T. (2006). A history of the disability rights movement in South Africa. In B. Watermeyer, L. Swartz, L., T. Lorenzo, M. Schneider, & M. Priestley (Eds.), *Disability and social change: A South African agenda* (pp. 46–98). Cape Town: HSRC Press.

Human Rights Watch (2019). Ghana: Faith healers defy ban on chaining. Available at: https://www.hrw.org/news/2019/11/27/ghana-faith-healersdefy-ban-chaining (Accessed April 6, 2020).

Igbinomwanhia, N. G., & Omoaregba, J. O. (2013). The attitudes of clergy in Benin City, Nigeria towards persons with mental Illness. *African Journal of Psychiatry, 16*, 196–200. Available at: https//doi.org/10.4314/ajpsy.v16i3.26. PMID: 23739822.

Iliffe, J. (1987). *The African poor. A history*. Cambridge: Cambridge University Press.

Ingham, G. (1964). Training of blind women. *Advance, 43*(July), 31–33.

Ingstad, B. (1990). *The disabled person in the community: Social and cultural aspects. International Journal of Rehabilitation Research, 13*, 187–194.

Innstrand, S. T., Espnes, G. A., & Mykletun, R. (2002). Burnout among people working with intellectually disabled persons: A theory update and an example. *Scandinavian Journal of Caring Sciences, 16*(3), 272–279. Available at: https://doi.org/10.1046/j.1471-6712.2002.00084.x

Jolley, E., Lynch, P., Virendrakumar, B., Rowe, S., & Schmidt, E. (2017). Education and social inclusion of people with disabilities in five countries in West Africa: A literature review. *Disability and Rehabilitation*. Available at: https://doi.org/10.1080/09638288.2017.1353649

Karna, G. (1999). *United Nations and the rights of disabled persons: A study in Indian perspective*. Society for disability and rehabilitation studies. New Delhi: A.P.H.

Kassah, A. K. (2008). Begging as work: A study of people with mobility difficulties in Accra, Ghana. *Disability & Society, 23*(2), 163–170. Available at: http://dx.doi.org/10.1080/09687590701841208

Kassah, A. K., Kassah, B. L. L., & Agbota, T. K. (2012). Abuse of disabled children in Ghana. *Disability and Society, 27*, 689–701. Available at: https://doi.org/10.1080/09687599.2012.673079

Kassah, A. K., Kassah, B. L. L., & Agbota, T. K. (2014). Abuse of physically disabled women in Ghana: Its emotional consequences and coping strategies. *Disability & Rehabilitation, 36*(8), 665–671.

Ker, R. (2013). *Challenging the ethnocentric bias in psychology: A counselling psychologist's perspective*. Unpublished Doctoral Thesis. London: City University.

Kerr, N. A., & Stanley, T. (2020). Revisiting the social stigma of loneliness. *Personality and Individual Differences, 171*(3), 110482. Available at: https://doi.org/10.1016/j.paid.2020.110482

Kim, D. (2017). Relationships between caregiving stress, depression, and self-esteem in family caregivers of adults with a disability. *Occupational Therapy International, 17*, 1686143. Available at: https://doi.org/10.1155/2017/1686143.

Kisanji, J. (1995). Attitudes and beliefs about disability in Tanzania. In B. O'Toole & R. McConkey (Eds.), *Innovations in developing countries for people with disabilities* (pp. 51–70). Baltimore: Paul H. Brookes.

Kittay, E. F. (2011). The ethics of care, dependence and disability. *An International Journal of Jurisprudence and Philosophy of the Law, 24*(1), 49–58.

Kiyaga, N. B., & Moores, D. F. (2003). Deafness in Sub-Saharan Africa. *American Annals of the Deaf, 148*, 18–24.

Kpobi, L. N., & Swartz, L. (2019). Muslim traditional healers in Accra, Ghana: Beliefs about and treatment of mental disorders. *Journal of Religion and Health, 58*(3), 833–846. Available at: https://doi.org/10.1007/s10943-018-0668-1

Kroeber, A. L., & Kluckhohn, C. (1952). Culture: A critical review of concepts and definitions. *Harvard University Peabody Museum of American Archeology and Ethnology Papers 47.*

Kudlick, C. J. (2003). Disability history: Why we need another "other." *The American Historical Review, 108*(3), 763–793.

Kurin, R. (2004). Safeguarding Intangible Cultural Heritage in the 2003 UNESCO Convention: a critical appraisal. *International, 56*(1–2), 66–77. Available at: https://doi.org/10.1111/j.1350-0775.2004.00459.x

Kuvalekar, K., Kamath, R., Ashok, L., Shetty, B., Mayya, S., & Chandrasekaran, V. (2015). Quality of life among persons with physical disability in Udupi Taluk: A cross sectional study. *Journal of Family Medicine and Primary Care, 4*(1), 69–73. Available at: https://doi.org/10.4103/2249-4863.152258

Lambert, J. E., Nantogmah, F., Dokurugu, A. Y., Alhassan, H., Azuure, S. S., Yaro, P. B., & Korner, J. (2020). The treatment of mental illness in faith-based and traditional healing centres in Ghana: Perspectives of service users and healers. *Global Mental Health, 7*(1), 1–8. Available at: https://doi.org/10.1017/gmh.2020.21

Lamptey, D. L. (2019). Health beliefs and behaviours of families towards the health needs of children with intellectual and developmental disabilities (IDD) in Accra, Ghana. *Journal of Intellectual Disability Research, 63*(1), 12–20. Available at: https://doi.org/10.1111/jir.12545

Link, B. G., & Phelan, J. C. (2001). Conceptualizing stigma. *Annual Review of Sociology, 27*(1), 363–385.

Liu, M. (2016). Family, religion and psychiatry in Ghana. *Perspectives in Global Mental Health.* Available at: https://doi.org/10.1176/appi.ajp-rj.2016.110806

Livingston, J. (2005). *Debility and the moral imagination in Botswana.* Bloomington: Indiana University Press.

Livingston, J. (2006). Insights from an African history of disability. *Radical History Review, 94*, 111–126.

Longmore, P., & Umansky, L., Eds. (2001). *The new disability history: American perspectives.* New York: New York University Press.

Lord, J., Posarac, A., Nicoli, M., Peffley, K., Mcclain-Nhlapo, C., & Keogh, M. (2010). *Disability and international cooperation and development: A review of policies and practices.* Washington DC: Social Protection and Labor, The World Bank.

Lord, J., & Stein, M. A. (2013). Prospects and practices for CRPD implementation in Africa. *African Disability Rights Yearbook, 1*, 97–113.

Lyons, C., Hopley, P., & Horrocks, J. (2009). A decade of stigma and discrimination in mental health: Plus ca change, plus c'est la meme chose (the more things change, the more they stay the same). *Journal of Psychiatric and Mental Health Nursing, 16*, 501–507. Available at: https://doi.org/10.1111/j.13652850.2009.01390.x

Magwaza, T. S. C. (2004). Towards a contemporary understanding and relevance of Zulu Proverbs. *Southern African Journal of Folklore, 14*(1), 32–41.

Malinga, J. T. (1999). The Pan-African movement of people with disabilities. In B. Holzer, A. Vreede, and G. Weigt (Eds.), *Disability in different cultures: Reflections on local concepts* (pp. 274–276). New Brunswick: Transaction.

Mamah, V., Deku, P., Darling, S. M., & Avoke, S. K. (2011). University teachers' perception of inclusion of visually impaired in Ghanaian Universities. *International Journal of Special Education, 26*(1), 70–79.

Mantey, E. F. (2017). Discrimination against children with disabilities in mainstream schools in Southern Ghana: Challenges and perspectives from stakeholders. *International Journal of Educational Development*, *54*(May), 18–25.

Manulife (2014). *What is stigma?* Available at: https://www.manulife.ca/business/mental-wellness-solutions/understanding-mental-health/stigma.html

Marfo, K., Walker, S., & Charles, B. I., Eds. (1983). *Education and rehabilitation of the disabled in Africa.* Edmonton: Centre for International Education & Development, University of Alberta.

Mbiti, J. (1969). *African religions and philosophies* (Second edition). London: Heinemann.

Mbiti, J. S. (1991). *Introduction to African religion* (2nd ed.). London: Heinemann Educational Books.

Mead, M. (2002). *Cooperation and competition among primitive peoples*. Routledge.

Meekosha, H. (2008). *Contextualizing disability: Developing South/Global Theory.* Keynote paper given to 4th Biennial Disability Studies Conference, Lancaster University, UK, September 2–4. Available at: www.wwda.org.au/wp-content/uploads/2013/12/meekosha2008.doc.

Mensah, E. O. (2017). Proverbs in Nigerian pidgin. *Journal of Anthropological Research, 69*(1), 87–115. Available at: https://www.jstor.org/stable/24393641

Mensah, S. A., Badu, E., & Opoku, M. P. (2015). Towards an inclusive society in Ghana: An analysis of challenges persons with disabilities face in participating in tourism in the Ashanti Region. *Journal of Social Inclusion, 6*(2), 64–76.

Metts, R. (2004). *Disability and development.* Background Paper Prepared for the Disability and Development Research Agenda Meeting, November 16, 2004. Washington, DC: World Bank.

Meyer, C. (2017). *Communicating for results: A Canadian student's guide* (4th ed.). Oxford: Oxford University Press.

Mfoafo-M'Carthy, M., & Grischow, J. D. (2017). Mental illness, stigma and disability rights in Ghana. *African Disability Rights Yearbook, 5*:84–100.

Mfoafo-M'Carthy, M., & Grischow, J. D. (2021). "Hope deferred": Meeting the challenges of mental health stigma in Ghana. *Social Work in Mental Health*. Available at: http://dx.doi.org/10.1080/15332985.2021.1996504

Mfoafo-M'Carthy, M., & Grischow, J. D. (2022). Mental health patients in Ghana share their stories about stigma and suffering. *The Conversation*. Available at: https://theconversation.com/mental-health-patients-in-ghana-share-their-stories-about-stigma-and-suffering-172689

Mfoafo-M'Carthy, M., & Sossou, M. (2017). Stigma, discrimination, and social exclusion of the mentally ill: The case of Ghana. *Journal of Human Rights and Social Work*. Available at: https://doi.org/10.1007/s41134-0170043-2

Mfoafo-M'Carthy, M., Grischow, J. D., & Stocco, N. (2020). Cloak of invisibility: A literature review of physical disability in Ghana. *Sage Open*. Available at: https://doi.org/10.1177/2158244019900567

Miles, M. (n.d.). Disability in Africa: Healing, spirituality, religious & ethical responses, to and by People with Disabilities, Deafness or Mental Debility: A bibliography through four millennia, with introduction and partial annotation. Available at: https://www.researchgate.net/publication/322283187_DISABILITY_IN_AFRICAabs

Miles, M. (2004). Locating deaf people, gesture and sign in African histories, 1450s–1950s. *Disability & Society, 19*(5), 531–545.

Miles, S. (1996). Engaging with the disability rights movement: The experience of community-based rehabilitation in southern Africa. *Disability & Society, 11*(4), 501–517.

Ministry of Gender, Children and Social Protection, Ghana. (2015b). Livelihood empowerment against poverty (LEAP). Available at: http://mogcsp.gov.gh/projects/livelyhood-empowerment-against-poverty-leap/

Mitra, S., Posarac, A., & Vick, B. (2011). *Disability and poverty in developing countries: A snapshot from the world health survey*. SP Discussion Paper No. 1109: Washington, DC: The World Bank.

Mkabile, S., Garrun, K. L., Shelton, M., & Swartz, L. (2021). African families' and caregivers' experiences of raising a child with intellectual disability: A narrative synthesis of qualitative studies. *African Journal of Disability, 10*, 827. Available at: https://doi.org/10.4102%2Fajod.v10i0.827

Moasun, F. (2019). *Exploring the personhood and citizenship of persons with disabilities among Konkombas in Rural Ghana*. Doctoral Dissertation, Wilfrid Laurier University. Available at: https://scholars.wlu.ca/etd/2238/

Moasun, F. Y. (2023). Deconstructing disability from a global south perspective: Examples from an interpretive phenomenological study. In C. Riegel & K. M. Robinson (Eds.), *Health humanities in application*. Cham: Palgrave MacMillan.

Moasun, F. Y., & Mfoafo-M'Carthy, M. (2021). The power of the tongue: Inherent labeling of persons with disabilities in proverbs of the Akan people of Ghana. *Qualitative Social Work*. Available at: https://doi.org/10.1177/1473325020910469

Momene, R. (2015). *Negative stereotypes and Attitudes Linked with Disability*. Atlas Corps. Available at: https://atlascorps.org/negative-stereotypes-and-attitudes-linked-to-disability/

Mprah, W. K., & Duorinaah, J. (2022). Knowledge and utilization of the CRPD and persons with disability Act 715 of Ghana among deaf people. In J. Grischow & M. Mfoafo-M'Carthy, *Disability rights and inclusiveness in Africa: The convention on the rights of persons with disabilities, challenges and change* (pp. 171–192). London: James Currey.

Naami, A. (2015). Disability, gender, and employment relationships in Africa: The case of Ghana. *African Journal of Disability, 4*(1), 1–11.

Naami, A., & Hayashi, R. (2012). Perceptions about disability among Ghanaian University students. *Journal of Social Work in Disability & Rehabilitation, 11*(2), 100–111.

Naami, A., & Okine, J. (2022). CRPD Article 6 – Vulnerabilities of women with disabilities. In J. Grischow & M. Mfoafo-M'Carthy, *Disability rights and inclusiveness in Africa: The convention on the rights of persons with disabilities, challenges and change* (pp. 193–210). London: James Currey.

National Health Insurance Authority, Ghana (2013). *2013 annual report*. Accra: NHIA.

Ndetei, D. M., et al. (2016). Stigmatizing attitudes toward mental illness among primary school children in Kenya. *Social Psychiatry and Psychiatric Epidemiology, 51*, 79.

Nepveux, M. D. (2009). *"In the same soup": Marginality, vulnerability and belonging in life stories of disabled Ghanaian women* (Doctoral Thesis). Available at: http://hdl.handle.net/10027/18451

Nutli, E., & Traore, M. (2013). A study of Ghanaian early childhood teachers' perceptions about inclusive education. *Journal of the International Association of Special Education, 14*(1), 50–57.

Nukunya, G. K. (2003). *Tradition and change in Ghana: An introduction to sociology* (2nd ed.). Accra: Ghana Universities Press.

Obeng, C. (2007). Teacher's views on the teaching of children with disabilities in Ghanaian classrooms. *International Journal of Special Education, 22*(1), 96–102.

Oliver, M. (1990). *The individual and social models of disability: Reader in disability studies*. London: Thames Polytechnic.

Oliver, M. (2004). The social model in action: If I had a hammer. In C. Barnes & G. Mercer (Eds.), *Implementing the social model of disability: Theory and research* (pp. 18–31). Leeds: The Disability Press.

Opare-Henaku, A., & Utsey, S. O. (2017). Culturally prescribed beliefs about mental illness among the Akan of Ghana. *Transcult Psychiatry, 54*(4), 502–522. Available at: https://doi.org/10.1177/1363461517708120

Opoku, M. P., Alupo, B. A., Gyamfi, N., Odame, L., Mprah, W. K., Torgbenu, E. L., & Badu, E. (2017). The family and disability in Ghana: Highlighting gaps in achieving social inclusion. *Disability, CBR and Inclusive Development, 28*(4), 41–59. Available at: https://doi.org/10.5463/dcid.v28i4.666

Oppong-Ansah, A. (2011). Deformed children are being killed. Available at: https://ghananewsagency.org/features/deformed-children-are-being-killed-in-ghana-34633

Osafo, J. (2016). Seeking paths for collaboration between religious leaders and mental health professionals in Ghana. *Pastoral Psychology, 65*, 493–508.

Palmer, H. R. (1928). The Kano Chronicle. In *Sudanese Memoirs* (3 vols, reprinted (1967) as one volume, vol. III, pp. 101–110). London: Cass.

Patton, M. Q. (2002). *Qualitative evaluation and research methods* (3rd ed.). London: SAGE.

Rajati, F., Ashtarian, H., Salari, N., Ghanbari, M. Naghibifar, Z., & Hosseini, S. Y. (2018). Quality of life predictors in physically disabled people. *Journal of Education and Health Promotion, 7*, 61. Available at: https://doi.org/10.4103/jehp.jehp_115_17

Read, U. M. (2016). Madness and miracles: Hoping for healing in rural Ghana. In K. Littlewood & R. Lynch (Eds.), *Cosmos, gods and madmen: Frameworks in anthropologies of medicine* (pp. 45–66). New York: Berghan Books.

Read, U. M. (2019). Rights as relationships: Collaborating with faith healers in community mental health in Ghana. *Culture, Medicine, and Psychiatry: An International Journal of Cross-Cultural Health Research, 43*(4), 613–635. Available at: https://doi.org/10.1007/s11013-019-09648-3

Read, U. M., Adiibokah, E., & Nyame, S. (2009). Local suffering and the global discourse of mental health and human rights: An ethnographic study of responses to mental illness in rural Ghana. *Globalization and Health, 5*(13), 1–16. Available at: https://doi.org/10.1186/1744-8603-5-13

Regehr, C., & Glancy, G. (2021). *Mental health social work practice in Canada* (3rd ed.). Toronto: Oxford University Press.

Retief, M., & Letšosa, R. (2018). Models of disability: A brief overview. *HTS Teologiese Studies/ Theological Studies, 74*(1), a4738. Available at: https://doi.org/10.4102/hts.v74i1.4738

Reynolds, S. (2010). Disability culture in West Africa: Qualitative research indicating barriers and progress in the Greater Accra region of Ghana. *Occupational Therapy International, 17*(4), 198–207.

Ridley, H. (1945). *Ocular onchocerciasis, including an investigation in the gold coast.* London: George Pulman and Sons.

Ritsher, J. B., & Phelan, J. C. (2004). Internalized stigma predicts erosion of morale among psychiatric outpatients. *Psychiatric Research, 129*, 257–265. Available at: https://doi.org/10.1016/j.psychres.2004.08.003

Rokach, A., Lechcier-Kimel, R., & Safarov, A. (2006). Loneliness of people with physical disabilities. *Social Behavior and Personality: An International Journal, 34*, 681–700.

Russell, M. (2002). What disability civil rights cannot do: Employment and political economy. *Disability & Society, 17*(2), 118–130.

Russell, M., & Malhotra, R. (2002). Capitalism and disability. *Socialist Register, 38*, 211–228.

Sackey, E. (2015). Disability and political participation in Ghana: An alternative perspective. *Scandinavian Journal of Disability Studies, 17*(4), 366–381.

Sadowsky, J. (1999). *Imperial bedlam: institutions of madness in colonial southwest Nigeria.* Berkeley: University of California Press.

Scalenghe, S. (2014). *Disability in the Ottoman Arab World, 1500-1800.* New York: Cambridge University Press.

Scalenghe, S. (2018). Physical disabilities in the premodern Arab World. In C. Kudlick, K. Nielsen, & M. Rembis (Eds.), *Oxford handbook of disability history* (pp. 71–84). New York: Oxford University Press.

Setume, S. D. (2016). Myths and beliefs about disabilities: Implications for educators and counselors. *Journal of Disability & Religion, 20*(1–2), 62–76. Available at: https://doi.org/10.1080/23312521.2016.1152938

Silván-Ferrero, P., Recio, P., Molero, F., & Nouvilas-Pallejà, E. (2020). Psychological quality of life in people with physical disability: The effect of internalized stigma, collective action and resilience. *International Journal of Environmental Research and Public Health, 17*(5). Available at: https://doi.org/10.3390/ijerph17051802

Silverman, D. (2015). *Interpreting qualitative data: A guide to the principles of qualitative research* (5th ed.). London: SAGE.

Slikker, J. (2009). *Attitudes towards persons with disability in Ghana.* Ghana: Voluntary Service Overseas (VSO).

Smeets, R. (2004). Language as a vehicle of the intangible cultural heritage. *Museum International, 56*(1–2), 156–165. Available at: https://doi.org/10.1111/j.1350-0775.2004.00470.x

Sottie, C. A., Mfoafo-M'Carthy, M., & Moasun, F. (2018). Graduate social work students' perceptions and attitude toward mental illness: Implications for practice in developing countries, *Social Work in Mental Health.* Available at: https://doi.org/10.1080/15332985.2018.1448325

Spittel, S., Maier, A., & Kraus, E. (2018). Awareness challenges of mental health disorder and dementia facing stigmatisation and discrimination: a systematic literature review from Sub-Sahara Africa. *Journal of Global Health, 9*(2). Available at: https://doi.org/10.7189/jogh.09.020419

Stone-MacDonald, A., & Butera, G. (2012). Cultural beliefs and attitudes about disability in East Africa. *Review of Disability Studies, 8*(1). Available at: http://www.rdsjournal.org/index.php/journal/issue/view/v8i1/showToc

Sue, D. W. (n.d). *Microaggression: More than just race.* Available at: https://www.uua.org/files/pdf/m/microaggressions_by_derald_wing_sue_ph.d._.pdf

Sue, D. W., Capodilupo, C. M., Torino, G. C., Bucceri, J. M., Holder, A. M. B., Nadal, K. L., & Esquilin, M. (2007). Racial microaggressions in everyday life: Implications for clinical practice. *American Psychologist, 62*(4), 271–286. Available at: https://doi.org/10.1037/0003-066X.62.4.271

Sullivan, K. (2011). *The prevalence of the medical model of disability in society.* AHS Capstone Projects. Paper 13. Available at: http://digitalcommons.olin.edu/ahs_capstone_2011/13

Talle, A. (1995). A Child is a child: Disability and equality among the Kenya Maasai. In B. Ingstad & S. R. Whyte (Eds.), *Disability and culture* (pp. 56–72). Berkley: University of California Press.

Tawiah, P. E. (2012). *Stigma and discriminations suffered by mental patients and their caregivers in the Ho municipality of Ghana*. PhD Dissertation, University of Ghana.

Taylor, C. (1985). *Philosophical papers: Human agency and language* (vol. 1). Cambridge: Cambridge University Press.

Teklemariam, A. A. (2010). Ethical Issues in the Abyssinian Customary Practices and Attitudes towards Persons with Mental or Physical Challenges. *Western Journal of Black Studies, 34*(1), 36–42.

Thompson, L. A., & Qualls, S. (2015). *Emmanuel's dream: The true story of Emmanuel Ofosu Yeboah*. New York: Schwartz and Wade Books.

Thornicroft, G., et al. (2007). Discrimination in health care against people with mental illness. *International Review of Psychiatry, 19*, 113–114.

Trani, J. F., Moodley, J., Anand, P., Graham. L., & Thu Maw, M. T. (2020). Stigma of persons with disabilities in South Africa: Uncovering pathways from discrimination to depression and low self-esteem. *Social Science & Medicine, 265*, 113449. Available at: https://doi.org/10.1016/j.socscimed.2020.113449

Tremearne, A. J. N. (1913). The boy who refused to walk. In A. J. N. Tremearne, *Hausa superstitions and customs* (pp. 351–354). London: Bale, Sons & Danielsson.

Twumasi, P. A. (1979). Community involvement in health care: The Kintampo experience in Ghana A study in the changing health model. *Ghana Medical Journal, 13*, 80–84.

Union of the Physically Impaired Against Segregation (1976). *Fundamental principles of disability*. London: UPIAS.

United Nations (1971). *Declaration on the rights of mentally retarded persons*. Available at: http://www.ohchr.org/Documents/ProfessionalInterest/res2856.pdf/

United Nations (1975). *Declaration on the rights of disabled persons*. Available at: http://www.ohchr.org/Documents/ProfessionalInterest/res3447.pdf/

United Nations (2006). *Convention on the rights of persons with disabilities*. New York: General Assembly of the United Nations. Available at: http://www.un.org/disabilities/documents/convention/convoptprot-e.pdf/

United Nations (2015). *United Nations Convention on the Rights of Persons with Disabilities (CRPD) infographic*. Available at: http://www.un.org/disabilities/documents/COP/cosp8_infographic.pdf

United Nations Children's Fund [UNICEF] (n.d). *Reducing stigma and discrimination against children with disabilities*. UNICEF. Available at: https://www.unicef.org/media/120421/file/Social_and_Behavioural_Change_Interventions_to_Strengthen_Disability_Inclusive_Programming_Summary.pdf

United Nations Division for Social Policy Development, and Department of Economic and Social Affairs (n.d.). *Toolkit on disability in Africa: Culture, beliefs, and disability*. UNDSPD & UNDESA. Available at: https://www.un.org/esa/socdev/documents/disability/Toolkit/Cultures-Beliefs-Disability.pdf

United Nations Educational, Scientific and Cultural Organization (2003). *Text of the convention for the safeguarding of the intangible cultural heritage*. Available at: https://ich.unesco.org/en/convention.

Virendrakumar, B., Stephen, C., Jolley, E., & Schmidt, E. (2021). *Disability-related stigma and discrimination in sub-Saharan Africa and south Asia: A systematic literature review*. Sightsavers. Available at: https://research.sightsavers.org/wp-content/uploads/2021/08/Sightsavers-systematic-review-into-stigma-and-disability-FINAL-UPDATED.pdf

Voice Ghana (2014). *Political governance for persons with disabilities: A study on the level of participation of persons with disabilities in local governance*. Available at: http://www.voiceghana.org/downloads/Research%20on%20Political%20Governance%20for%20PWDs.pdf

Walker, R. (2014). *The shame of poverty*. Oxford Academic. Available at: https://doi.org/10.1093/acprof:oso/9780199684823.003.0005

Walker, S. (1975). *The disabled in Ghana: Status and change in information and attitude*. PhD Dissertation, Columbia University.

Wilson, J. W. (1961). *Ghana's handicapped citizens*. Accra: Government Printer.

Wilson, J. W. (1963). *Travelling blind*. London: Hutchinson & Co.

World Bank (2011). Ghana looks to retool its economy as it reaches middle-income status. Available at: https://www.worldbank.org/en/news/feature/2011/07/18/ghana-looks-to-retool-its-economy-as-it-reaches-middle-income-status

World Bank (2023). Population, total – Ghana. Available at: https://data.worldbank.org/indicator/SP.POP.TOTL?locations=GH

World Health Organization (2004). CBR: A strategy for rehabilitation, equalization of opportunities, poverty reduction and social inclusion of people with disabilities. Joint position paper with the International Labour Organization, the United Nations Educational, Scientific and Cultural Organization and the World Health Organization. Washington, WHO.

World Health Organization (2013). *Comprehensive mental health action plan 2013–2020*. Geneva: World Health Organization. Available at: http://apps.who.int/gb/ebwha/pdf_files/WHA66/A66_R8-en.pdf?ua=1

World Health Organization (2014). Mental health: A state of well-being. Available at: http://www.who.int/features/factfiles/mental_health/en/

World Health Organization (2017). Mental disorders: Fact sheet. Available at: http://www.who.int/mediacentre/factsheets/fs396/en/

World Health Organization (2023). Disability. Available at: https://www.who.int/health-topics/disability#tab=tab_1

World Health Organization and World Bank (2011). *World Report on Disability*. Geneva: World Health Organization.

Yendork, S., Brew, J., Beryl, G., Sarfo, E. A., & Kpobi, L. (2018). Mental illness has multiple causes: Beliefs on causes of mental illness by congregants of selected neo-prophetic churches in Ghana. *Mental Health, Religion & Culture, 21*(7), 647–666. Available at: https://doi.org/10.1080/13674676.2018.1511694

Zuurmond, M., Nyante, G., Baltussen, M., Seeley, J., Abanga, J., Shakespeare, T., & Bernays, S. (2018). A support programme for caregivers of children with disabilities in Ghana: Understanding the impact on the wellbeing of caregivers. *Child: Care, Health and Development, 45*(1), 1–9. Available at: https://doi.org/10C.1111/cch.12618

Index

Accra Rehabilitation Center (ARC), 24, 28, 29, 31
Achebe, C., 44
Ad Hoc Committee (AHC), 30
Agbenyega, J. S., 43, 47, 49, 54
aggression, 6, 52
Akan ethnic group, 11
Akropong School for Blind, 27
Alem, A., 73
Alhassan, A. K., 61
Amedome, S. N., 73
Amoako, J. B., 25
angular kyphosis, 20, 45, 75
Ansong, L., 24
Appiah, P., 44, 45
Asamoa, P. O., 13
Ayagiyire, T., 47

Baffoe, M., 43
Baker, C., 55
Bedi, I. K., 73
Bikpakpaam Elders, 47
Birukou, A., 40
Bolle, K. W., 54
Braun, V., 10
British Council of Organizations of Disabled People (BCDOP), 26
British Empire Society for the Blind (BESB), 23, 34

caregivers. *See* family members and caregivers
causation, of disability: accidents, 79; medical illness/disease, 79–80; spiritual causes of, 80–81; stigma and discrimination, 81–83
Christians, 8, 9, 12, 22, 60–61, 65–67, 71, 73, 77, 127
Clarke, V., 10
community, 5–8, 19, 21–27, 29, 31, 41, 45, 59–62, 72, 76–78, 82–83, 88, 89, 94–96, 100, 101, 104–12, 123, 127, 128
Community Based Rehabilitation (CBR), 29
Convention on the Rights of Persons with Disabilities (CRPD), 7, 30
Convention People's Party (CPP), 23
corruption, 4
Creswell, J., 10
criminal justice system, 6
cultural identities, 12, 42, 126
culture and disability, in Ghana: characteristics, 40–41; disability stereotypes and myths, 50–56; indigenous beliefs, 46–50; language, 41–46

Daanaa, H. S., 13
data's validity, 10
deafness, 11, 15, 17–19, 34, 126
degradation, 5, 28, 81
denial of right to marry, 84–85
Despouy, L., 30
developmental disabilities, 25, 30, 35
Devlieger, P. J., 42, 47–49
Disability Act, 31, 34, 122
disability research, in Ghana: beliefs about mental illness, 119–20; culture and belief systems, 119; kinship, 122–23; policy gaps, 120–22
disability stigma, in Ghana, 7–9; abuse and neglect of persons, 88–90; accepting situation, 108; cultural norms and beliefs, 12; and culture (*see* culture and disability, in Ghana); denial of right, 13; denial of right to marry, 84–85; and discrimination, 76–78; emotional and psychological impact, 102–5; experience of disrespect, 87–88; family members and caregivers, 92–93, 101–2, 107; family members' direct experiences, 93–5; history of (*see* history, of disability in Ghana); labeling and name-calling, 84; marriage partners, 95–96, 99–101; non-African religions, 12; organized religion, 12; overbearing care responsibilities, 105–7; personhood, 97–98; public's negative perceptions, 84; religion and spiritual beliefs, 12; research methodology, 9–11; spiritual beliefs, 13; stereotypes, 84; unconscious bias, 85–86; well-being of women, 4
Disabled People's International (DPI), 26
discrimination, 5, 6; abuse and neglect of persons with disabilities, 88–90; community level, 6; cultural and social discrimination, 30; and disability stigma (*see* disability stigma, in Ghana); discriminatory response, 6; experience of disrespect, 87–88; marriage-related stigma, 95–96; by public stigma, 6; stereotyping and prejudice, 6; society's perception of, 77
District Assembly Common Fund, 89
Dotse, P., 24
double stigmatization, 126

Edwards, J., 63
emotional and psychological impact, 128; feelings of pain, 102–3; frustrations, 105; isolation and loneliness, 103–5; sorrow and sadness, 102–3
Encyclopedia Britannica, 50
epilepsy, 43, 48, 61, 83

family members and caregivers, 9, 92–93, 93–95, 101–2, 107; of indirect stigma and discrimination, 96–97; labeling and name-calling, 94–95; social exclusion and loss of friends, 93–94
Federation of Disabled Associations (FODA), 29
feelings of pain, 128
Fefoame, G., 13
Fiasorgbor, A. D., 47
financial barriers, 33
Foster, Andrew, 23
Foucault, M., 52

Geurts, Kathryn, 24
Ghana: disability research (*see* disability research, in Ghana); elderly, 4; faith-based healing center in, 62; inequality, 4; religion and spirituality in, 73; socioeconomic and cultural overview, 4; well-being of women, 4
Ghana Association of the Blind (GAB), 24
Ghana Department of Social Welfare, 27
Ghana Education Service (GES), 27, 29
Ghana Federation of the Disabled (GFD), 29

Ghana Society of the Physically Disabled (GSPD), 28
Ghana Statistical Service, 122
Global South, 3, 41, 91, 118
God: belief in, 66–67; dependence on, 70–71; leave things to, 108–9
Grischow, J., 32

Hanlon, C., 73
healthcare system, 6
health conditions, 3
hearing and speech impairments, 54, 55
history, of disability in Ghana: colonial Ghana, 22–23; in independent Ghana I, 23–25; in independent Ghana II, 25–33; precolonial period, 17–22
Holder, S. M., 84
Home and School for Children, 27
human rights, 27
human rights violations, 31, 62

Imafidon, E., 55
Inclusive Education (IE), 30
indigenous beliefs, 12
Industrial Rehabilitation Center in Accra, 27
institutionalization, 64–66, 127
institutionalized religion, 71–72
International Decade of Disabled People, 26
international human rights, 31
International Labor Organization, 25
International Year of Disabled People (IYDP), 25, 27

Kluckhohn, C., 40
Kpobi, L. N., 60
Kroeber, A. L., 40
Kurin, R., 42

Lambert, J. E., 63
Livelihood Empowerment Against Poverty, 120
Lord, J., 118

Magwaza, T. S. C., 44
Mampong School for Deaf, 27
Mampong Teacher Training Centre, 27
marginalization, 3, 43, 50, 52, 54, 56, 57, 71, 103, 126, 127
material realm, 127
medical and social rehabilitation, 35
Meekosha, H., 118
mental and psychological impairments, 3
Mental Health Bill into law (Act 846), 120
mental illness, 84, 120, 125–27; alcohol and marijuana, 64–65; causation of disability and, 79–83; discriminated against in workplace, 8; god and accepting, 67–70; misconception of, 53; moral explanations for, 61; and physical disabilities, 7; in precolonial Akan societies, 21; religion and spirituality, 64–71, 127; stereotypes of, 53
Meyer, C., 40
Mfoafo-M'Carthy, M., 44
Ministries of Health and Education, 29
Ministry of Employment and Social Welfare, 29
Mitra, S., 118
Moasun, F., 44, 47
Momene, R., 50
Muslim African societies, 34
myths, 54–56

Naami, A., 43
National Disability Policy, 31
National Education Act, 24
National Health Insurance Authority (NHIA), 122
National Health Insurance Policy, 121
National Health Insurance Regulation, 121
National Health Insurance Scheme (NHIS), 120
National Social Protection Policy (NSPP), 120

negative beliefs, 6
negative stereotypes, 84
neoliberalism, 33
Nepveux, M. D., 118
Nkrumah, Kwame, 34, 125
Northern Ghana, 61
Norwegian Agency for Development Cooperation (NORAD), 29
Norwegian Association of the Disabled (NAD), 29
NVivo software, 10

Occupational Industrial Training Center, 27
ostracization, 3
Oxford Languages Dictionary, 50

Parents Association of Children with Intellectual Disabilities, 31
Participatory Action Research (PAR), 9
personhood, 48–49, 53, 57, 97–98
Persons with Disability Act (Act 715), 120, 122
physical impairments, 3, 46
Plahar, E., 28
political exclusion, 6
poverty, 119
private voluntary associations, 23
public stigma, 6

Quaye, Ben, 24

Rawlings, J. J., 28
Read, U. M., 62
rehabilitation approach, 11
Rehabilitation Department, 25
Rehabilitation International (RI) conference, 25
rehabilitation programs, 26, 32, 34
rehabilitation units, 23
religion: non-African religions, 12; organized religion, 12; and spirituality, 12, 64–71, 73, 127
research methodology, 9–11
Ridwan, A, 61
Rights and Voice Initiative (RAVI), 31
Rokach, A., 45
rural communities, 4
Rural Rehabilitation Training Centers, 27
Rural Rehabilitation Units, 23
Russell, Marta, 32

self-esteem, 84
self-determination, 32
self-sabotaging behavior, 7
self-stigma, 6, 7, 75; feelings of shame and embarassment, 84
semi-structured questionnaires, 9, 10
Sharecare Ghana, 31
Silverman, D., 10
Slikker, J., 48
Smeets, R., 42
snowball sampling technique, 116
social exclusion, 9, 128
social inclusion, 9, 34
social isolation, 8, 55, 126
social judgment, 5
social marginalization, 3
social model, 30
Social Sciences Research and Humanities Council of Canada (SSHRC), 9
social stigma, 84
social support, 3
Society for the Prevention of Tuberculosis, and St. Joseph's Hospital, 27
Society of Albinos Ghana, 31
Society of Friends of the Mentally Retarded Association (SFMRA), 25
Special Education Division, 29
special education initiatives, 29–30
Special Education Policy Act, 24
special education programs, 23
spirituality: and beliefs, 66, 118; and religion, 12, 64–71, 73, 127
State School for the Deaf, 27
stereotypes, 5, 50–53

stigma: definitions and parameters, 5–7; disability stigma (*see* disability stigma, in Ghana)
supernatural phenomena, 61, 62
Supreme Being, 61
Swartz, L., 60
Swedish Organizations of Disabled Persons International Aid Association (SHIA), 29

Twumasi, P. A., 62

UN Decade on Disability, 29
UN declarations, 25
underemployment, 8
UNESCO Convention for Safeguarding Intangible Cultural Heritage, 42
United Kingdom, 34
United Nations Children's Fund, 110
United Nations Convention on the Rights of Persons with Disabilities, 7
United Nations Educational, Scientific, and Cultural Organization (UNESCO), 41
University of Cape Coast, 27
UN's International Decade of Disabled Persons, 28
UN's Standard Rules, 31
urban and rural rehabilitation units, 23

verbal communication ability, 51
vocational training, 35
Vocational Training Rehabilitation Center, 27

Wilfrid Laurier University (WLU) Research Ethics Board, 10
Wilson, John, 23, 24
Winfrey, Oprah, 13
women: with hearing and speech impairments, 55; in rural communities, 116; well-being of, 4
World Bank, 4, 30, 75
World Health Organization (WHO), 3, 26, 60
World Program of Action Concerning Disabled Persons, 26
World Rehabilitation Fund (USA), 27
World War II, 34

Yeboah, Emmanuel, 13
Young Men's Christian Association (YMCA), 27

About the Authors

Magnus Mfoafo-M'Carthy is a professor of social work at Wilfrid Laurier University in Canada. His research interests include global mental health, disability, and mental illness and stigma among immigrant communities. He is a former associate director of Wilfrid Laurier University's Tshepo Institute for the Study of Contemporary Africa (TISCA) and a former Carnegie African Diaspora fellow at the University of Ghana and the Ghana Institute of Management and Public Administration. He is involved in multiple collaborative projects in Canada, Ghana, and other parts of the world.

Jeff Grischow is an associate professor of history at Wilfrid Laurier University in Ontario, Canada. His research interests include the idea and practice of development in Africa and the history and experience of disability and disability rights in Ghana. His current research includes three projects with Magnus Mfoafo-M'Carthy supported by the Social Sciences and Humanities Research Council of Canada, which focus on disability rights and inclusive education in Ghana.

Festus Moasun is an assistant professor at the School of Social Work, University of Windsor. He specializes in (dis)ability and mental health in the Global South, immigrant populations, decoloniality, and politics of knowledge creation. He draws on critical qualitative methodologies including interpretive phenomenology, participatory action research, structured interview matrix, and digital ethnography for his research. Dr. Moasun is a Carnegie and Queen Elizabeth Scholar.

www.ingramcontent.com/pod-product-compliance
Ingram Content Group UK Ltd.
Pitfield, Milton Keynes, MK11 3LW, UK
UKHW041839031026
15587UKWH00002B/880

9 781666 905809